Publication Number
series of Outdoor Sp
from TARGET COM𝙽

ɪting

On Target for

Forty years in the black bear woods...

THE
BEAR HUNTING
OBSESSION
OF A DRIVEN MAN

by Bill Wiesner Jr.
with Glenn Helgeland

Library of Congress Control Number: 2015955916

TARGET COMMUNICATIONS
10459 N. Wauwatosa Rd.
Mequon, WI 53097

Printed in the United States of America
by Ripon Printers, Ripon, Wisconsin.

ISBN: 978-0-913305-11-9

TABLE OF CONTENTS

A NOTE FROM BILL WIESNER

I have been blessed with the urge, almost the need, to learn all I could about this magnificent animal, the black bear, *Ursus americanus*. Now, after more than four decades of writing about, filming, studying and pursuing bears, it is time to share in print what I've learned about black bears, enjoyed about black bears, plus my observations and conclusions regarding this wonderful game animal.

My goal is to help you better understand the black bear, to take you through every aspect of preparing to hunt it, and then hunting it, covering every existing black bear hunting method and technique, plus several new wrinkles I tried and learned from that, I believe, will help you in your bear hunting efforts.

I hope the information given opens doors for you to increased bear hunting enjoyment and success. So pour a cup of joe and enjoy. You just might come to agree with my description of a perfect day: to encounter more bears than people.

My passion for the black bear continues to grow. I want to learn everything I can about this magnificent animal. Knowing this pushes me farther into the bear's world. I look forward to the continued lessons.

ACKNOWLEDGEMENTS

Thank you to the people who influenced my life in a way that enables me to transfer my thoughts to print. The number is too large to put in print, but you know who you are.

The following need special mention:

Glenn Helgeland, editor and publisher of this book, because without his input this book never would have gotten off the ground. I do not care how knowledgeable you are, if you cannot transfer knowledge and thoughts, to the readers' benefit, your ideas remain solitary. Thank you for your help, Glenn.

My friend and bloodbrother Ted Nugent, who has always stood up for what is best for all outdoor people no matter how his thoughts and comments are received. His commitment to the outdoor experience has won my respect.

My family … wife Sandy, sons Brad and Bryan, their wives Nicole and Ashley, and my grandchildren, Tia, Keagan and Ryder. The good Lord has blessed me with the greatest gift of all, a loving family. Know that my love for all of you grows stronger every day.

DEDICATION

My dad taught me early in life that if something needed to be done, or you wanted to do a particular thing, do it! Therefore, the 'what if'" question has no room in my vocabulary. Not only did he earn my respect and love, my dad, William R. Wiesner Sr., is my hero. Whether I was on the wrestling mat or serving our country in the Marine Corps, Dad was there for me, spiritually if not always physically. That support inspired me.

I lost Dad in 2007, but his presence is felt every day, with every footstep I take in the bear woods and everywhere else.

PREFACE

GETTING AROUND AFIELD

I need a walking stick to get around in any woods. This isn't too bad in flat woods, but ridges, swamps, creek crossings and mountain terrain are added challenges. When I was younger I could walk all day. Now I can cover only a fraction of the distance I once could.

My left knee, left hip and back are in constant pain. I was injured while in the Marine Corps and received a 10 percent disability in 1972. At the time I could still get around very well, although it was painful.

As the effects from the injury progressed from my left knee to my hip and back because of the way I walked trying to protect my injured knee, things got much worse.

Bear hunting is my life, and I refuse to let an injury shut me down.

• Bear hunting is my life. I need a walking stick to get around in any woods, because I refuse to let an injury shut me down. This Wyoming hunt was a supreme challenge.

FAMILY INVOLVEMENT

Little did I know in 1962 where this whole bear thing was going to take me. Furthermore, how was I to know that my passion would eventually involve my wife, two sons and their wives, plus, Sandy and I have a granddaughter and two grandsons waiting in the wings.

In 1962, my first encounter with the black ghost of the north was a chance encounter. Since then, I have been many places with various members of our family-- sometimes one, sometimes all. After my hitch in the Marine Corps, I met Sandy and in 1972 we were married. She instantly showed interest in bear hunting. Since those early days, our bear hunts have been frequent and have taken us all over the United States and Canada. Her successful encounters have fit well in our bear hunting biography.

Family involvement is what it is all about, and the future for the Wiesner family looks great, bear-hunting-wise.

• The third generation of Wiesner bear hunters already is involved. Grandson Keagon watches granddaughter Tia spray me with a scent neutralizer to help me get ready for an evening hunt.

BearCrazy's Crazy Schedule in a Recent Bear Season
- **September 16**
  - Left Sturgeon Bay (WI) at 3:00 pm for son Bryan's cabin in Michiga UP (Upper Peninsula).

- **September 17**
  - Morning — Set up ground blinds for my grandson Keagan.
  - Noon - Drove back home to Sturgeon Bay for a 4:00 pm meeting manufacturing a bow for Freedom Hunters, an organization that provi hunts for disabled vets. Then went over what I need to film to promot 62-inch recurve bow and a 32-inch compound bow for Freedom Hun on YouTube.
  - Left Sturgeon Bay at 10:30 pm and drove to Spooner, WI.

- **September 18**
  - Arrived at Spooner hunting camp at 3:30 am, just in time to l locate fresh tracks for my granddaughter's bear hunt, a hunt with dogs. Tr searches are done in darkness with flashlight on sandy roads.
  - Hunted all day.

- **September 19**
  - Left at 7:00 am to go back to Iron River, MI, for my grandson's yc deer hunt.

TROPHY HUNTING ... OR NOT?

My family and I are bear hunters, not trophy bear hunters.   Any ac fully mature bear (190-225 pounds male, 120-150 pounds female) shooter bear, and any one of us will happily draw down on a bear of size or larger.

A 400-pound bear is really big; a 500-pound bear is exceptional, of course I will attempt to tag one that size when it arrives at my bait. Bearcrazy, not crazy.

Editor's Note On The Contents Of This Book

There is minor and unavoidable overlap and repetitiveness in some of topics in this book's contents ... spring and fall hunting guidelines, for insta in scouting, baiting, and stand set-up instructions. However, we came at e topic of this nature from different angles, a different set of priorities, for e chapter. Overall, this gives you a better and more complete view of the wh Various points were more pertinent in various chapters. There simply wa: way all points could be isolated into one chapter. They had too many tentac

We set up the book in the most logical chapter segments, trying to go f beginning to end of a hunt in the proper order of planning, preparation fulfillment.

We avoided needless duplication of some larger topics, such as bear anat and where to aim, by printing such subject matter in one chapter and, in o chapters, referring you to the first chapter listing when the subject matter relevant in subsequent chapters.

CHAPTER 1 - *Memoir*
LADY WITH THE MOUTH

SO YOU WANT TO BE A BEAR HUNTER

It was opening day of deer season. My nerves were as tight as violin strings, just like everyone else's on opening day. Had someone shouted 'BOO' behind me, I probably could have landed on the moon.

About 9:00 am I heard two shots in the swamp directly in front of me. I was instantly at full alert, waiting for the big swamp buck to come at me!

Instead, a red suit was making its way toward me. It was an elderly woman, chewing and spitting tobacco, swearing with every other word.

She laid a big wad of tobacco juice on the snow at my feet and asked, "What kind of a (expletive deleted) gun you shootin?

"A Remington 20-gauge pump," I said.

Her next words were more of an order than a statement.

"Follow me. My son Hermie just shot a bear."

As we entered the swamp, I noticed Hermie looking at the ground, but I could not see what he was looking at. Once we reached his location, I could see he was standing on a blood trail, a bear's blood trail.

The lady started barking orders like a drill instructor.

"Hermie take the (expletive deleted) blood trail. I will flank your right."

She turned to me. "You stay to his left. Be careful. We are dealing with a bear here."

She didn't need to tell me. My stomach was in knots. We slowly advanced on the trail. My eyes were trained straight ahead. We were in a tangle of alders, and it was difficult to see the other two red suits to my right.

Without warning, the bear jumped up right in front of me, maybe 10 yards away but no more.

I shot from the hip in pure reflexive, non-thinking, instant reaction. Had it been a red squirrel, I might have done the same.

The bear dropped. My shot had broken its spine.

"(Expletive deleted.) Hermie, you see that (expletive deleted) shot? Good job!"

Having a bear jump up in front of me at point blank range…incredible. It was heart stopping, unexpected, thrilling and any other emotion that could be layered on.

I thought the bear was a monster. OK, it weighed maybe 175 pounds; but you know how difficult it is to judge a bear's weight. That's why there's the infamous 'ground shrinkage' regarding bears seen and bears shot.

- - - - - -

I was 12 years old. This was my first day of deer hunting in my first season of deer hunting. I've not been the same since.

I have mentally thanked that foul-mouthed, brash old woman a thousand times for triggering my interest in bear hunting to such a degree that, over the years, it developed into a passion that continues to this day.

• *Back then (1962), it was legal to shoot bears during the Wisconsin firearms deer season and red was considered the proper safety color for your hunting jacket.*

Photo: Bill Wiesner

• *My obsession with black bear has become a family thing. From left, Bill, sons Brad and Bryan, wife Sandy, and guest of honor, taken with a longbow.*

CHAPTER 1 - How-To
WHAT IS THE BLACK BEAR?

WHERE BLACK BEARS LIVE

General

Throughout their North American range, black bear preferred habitats have a few shared characteristics–areas with relatively inaccessible terrain, thick understory and plenty of food, especially soft and hard masts. Adaptation to woodlands and thick vegetation may have originally been due to the black bear evolving alongside larger, more aggressive bear species that monopolized more-open habitats.

Black bears will always prefer heavy cover away from human population, but they are adapting to hybrid areas of fragmented urban and rural characteristics, as long as those regions contain easily accessible foods and adequate cover for security.

Regional habitats:

• Black bears in the southern Appalachian Mountains live in predominantly oak-hickory and mixed forests. This type of habitat is one of the most biologically diverse temperate regions on earth. It can have as many as 30 tree species at a single site. Along with the forest there is a rich undergowth of ferns, mushrooms, shrubs, herb-type plants and small trees as well as glades and bogs..

• In Southeastern coastal areas bears live in a mixture of pines, pine savannas, wiregrass, saw palmetto and swampy hardwood sites.

• In the Northeastern and Midwestern parts of the range (United States and Canada), prime habitat consists of a forest canopy of hardwoods such as beech, maple, birch and oak, and conifers. Corn crops and oak-hickory mast are also common sources of food in some sections of the Midwest and Northeast; small, thick, swampy areas provide excellent refuge cover largely

Photos: Bill/Sandy Wiesner

• **This is bear country, West . . .**   **Midwest and East.**

in stands of white cedar and alder.

• On the Pacific Coast, redwood, sitka spruce and hemlicks are primary tree cover, with lower cover such as fields of brush, wet and dry meadows, high tidelands, cover along rivers and streams, and a variety of mast-producing hardwood species.

• The spruce-fir forest dominates much of the bear's range in the Rocky Mountains, along with wet meadows, brush along and up-slope of streams, avalanche chutes, burns, sidehill parks and subalpine ridgetops.

• Where human development is low, such as in parts of Alaska and Canada, bears tend to be found more regularly in lowland regions. In parts of northeastern Canada, especially Labrador, black bears have adapted exclusively to semi-open areas. No other bear species live there.

See Chapter 5 – SCOUTING – for specific local habitats and terrain differences relative to placing bait sites and stands, and for spot-and-stalk hunting.

WHAT BLACK BEARS EAT

Black bears are omnivores, with their diets varying greatly depending on season and location. Somewhere from 75 percent to 90 percent of the protein in their diet comes from vegetable matter; the balance, 10 percent to 25 percent, is animal protein. Most studies have concluded closer to the 90/10 balance.

They are largely active during twilight (dawn and dusk) in foraging activities, though may actively feed at any time.

Diets vary with habitat, season and food supplies, of course. It's doubtful any individual bear's diet includes all entries on this list.

Vegetable Protein

As the spring temperature warms, black bears seek tender grasses, young shoots and buds of trees and shrubs, wetland plants and forbs. They also like fresh poplar tree buds and other softwood tree buds. This vegetation is especially important to black bears emerging from hibernation. They often are the only digestible foods available at that time. They help the bear's digestive system get into full gear again after a winter of complete inactivity.

During summer, the diet is largely berries and soft masts such as buds and

What is the Black Bear?

stone-fruits (plums, etc).

During the fall, when feeding is nearly the bear's full-time task, hard masts become the most important part of their diet, to such a point that several bears may feed in a small prime area. Favored hard masts (acorns and other nuts) may be consumed by the hundreds each day by a single bear during fall.

As is well known, once bears lose their fear of humans, they scavenge food at campgrounds and garbage dumps when natural foods are scarce. At a campground, you now have a problem bear. This is where most bear attacks occur.

Animal Protein

Black bears are not effective predators but will catch and eat deer fawns, elk calves, moose calves and beaver.

• *Bear diets are approximately 90% vegetable protein and 10% animal protein.*

Photo: Bill Wiesner

Bears eat honey, but more in folklore than in real life. Immature bees, which are mostly fat and protein, are much preferred. Honey does not compare to larvae in nutritional value. After eating, bears shake defending bees out of their heavy fur like a dog shakes off water.

Other animal protein comes from hornet larvae, tent caterpillars, grubs (especially June beetle grubs) and, in some areas, snow fleas. Bears occasionally find ground bird nests, eating eggs and younger hatchlihgs. They apparently don't like feathers in their mouth, and adult birds would be more difficult to catch. Nor do they like snakes, turtles, frogs, toads or salamanders.

Away from salmon areas, they seldom eat fish unless they find a stream with spawning suckers. One of the few places they eat fish remains is at campsites; fish remains on baits mostly draw flies.

When bears take deer fawns and elk calves as they are born, they first eat the high-fat milk in the fawn/calf stomach. Newborns are easy prey because a big part of their defense is to lie still. In roughly 10 days, when fawns develop scent and have grown enough to run, they escape easily. Black bears don't have the agility of dogs and cats to catch animals that are zigging and zagging.

Fresh and rotting carcasses in the summer are usually ignored, especially when nuts and berries are available. Bears will eat carcasses in spring and fall when they are available. However, scavengers usually have winter-kill carcasses cleaned up in the spring before bears come out of their dens, and they are in hibernation before deer entrails become available during hunting seasons in the fall. They break into beaver lodges to catch beaver.

Ant larvae and pupae, called a brood by biologists, are an important source of protein for bears from late spring to late summer over much of temperate North America. A bear's long, sticky tongue was made for probing into ant colonies. Ants are among the first solid foods cubs eat. Bears try to eat ant broods cleanly, without including soil, debris or adult ants, by most often looking under rocks, moss and ground litter.

Bears sniff along logs and stumps to locate ant colonies, then bite and claw into the colony. Worker ants immediately spray formic acid into the air and begin carrying off the brood. If bears don't work fast, worker ants can scatter the brood before the bears get to it. When researchers put their faces next to the bears' faces at logs (after first making sure the bear(s) being studied had accepted their continued presence), the researchers immediately learned the power of the odorous cloud of formic acid and jerked away.

Bears tend to avoid anthills and ant mounds unless food is scarce. Digging mixes too much soil with the brood. Bears don't add much fat when they must rely mainly on ant colonies and vegetation.

I did a field test 25 years ago. At a bait site, I placed half a salmon, a venison roast, some rotten beef and a mixture of breads and sweets. Breads and sweets were eaten first, followed by fresh meat, then fish, and way last the rotten meat. The age-old belief that bears like rotten, odorous meat is not true.

BEAR FOODS:
Berries & Fruits

• Wild strawberries	June		• Mulberries	June
• Currants	June		• Gooseberries	June
• Thimbleberries	June		• Raspberries	July
• Blueberries	July/Aug		• Blackberries	August
• Plums	August		• Cherries	Late June
• Choke Cherry	September		• Pin Cherry	Late June
• Cranberry	October		• Apples	Sept/Oct
• Wild Grapes	September		• Elderberries	September
• Hawthorne	Mid Oct		• Arrowwood	September
• Sarsaparilla	Late Summer		• Huckleberries	July-Sept
• Buffalo berries	Aug/Sept		• Aspen catkins	Spring
• Hazel nuts	September		• Poplar catkins	Spring
• Softwood tree buds	Spring			

Mast crops:

• Acorns	September		• Beech nuts	September
• Hazel nuts	October			

Farm Crops:

• Oats	July		• Corn	September

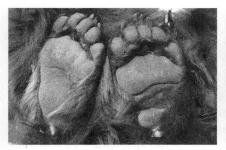

• *The front paw is somewhat square, the rear foot longer and narrower. A front paw of five inches or more width is a shooter bear. Bears lose the tough outer pad skin during hibernation, but it toughens up quickly again in the spring.*

• *This young, not very big bear rested comfortably away from the hounds. The ears look large compared to face size, and the head is narrow. The hound men and hunter took its picture before leaving the woods.*

Animal Protein:

- Larvae of bees, ants, hornets
- Elk calves
- Honey
- Lemmings (Labrador)
- Eggs & younger hatchlings
- Incidental moose calves
- Deer fawns
- Beaver
- Salmon
- Grubs
- Tent caterpillars

SKELETON & ANATOMY

• **See the center four-color section of this book for anatomical artwork.**

• **"Where to shoot" information is in Chapter 8 (The Shot – Before, During, After)**

• The black bear is a stocky, big-boned, heavily muscled animal, generally standing just over two feet to three feet at the shoulders.

• Bear ribs are narrower and thicker than deer ribs, almost half-moon shape in profile; they do not widen and flatten at the tips, as do deer ribs. Shoulder blades are thick in the middle and thicker yet near the edge, totally unlike deer shoulder blades. These two differences will be startling the first time you see them.

• The black bear has thick, coarse hair and thick underfur, a consideration when choosing a hunting gear set-up.

• The vitals, when the bear is broadside, extend back nearly to the mid-point of the body, and the liver is at mid-point. But the heart/lung area is the place to aim.

Basic Black Bear Body, Behaviorial & Additional Facts

• It is well known black bears have tremendous physical strength. They have been known to turn over flat rocks weighing more than 300 pounds by flipping them with one front leg and paw.

• They can run 25–30 mph, faster than a horse for a short distance.

• Black bears can do a lot with their front paws and claws. They can open screw-top jars and open door latches.

Mike Brust, a friend of the authors, told us about a bear eating the suet from suet cages in his back yaard. The suet was intended for birds, of course, and was in small wire cages that snap closed and are held to a back-plate by a couple of light metal tabs.

"Rose (his wife) watched a big bear eat the suet out of the suet feeder and then walk almost under our deck before sitting down. This bear had worked with suet feeders before. Other bears have ripped the suet cages off the back-plate and torn apart the cages. Not this guy. We have some big pileated woodpeckers that use the suet feeder and, because of their size their weight can open the cages. So Rose twist-ties the cages shut. This bear somehow removes the twist-ties and opens the cage doors without pulling the cages from the back-plates – and without opposing thumbs."

• Bears on the East Coast and Midest tend to average heavier than those on the West Coast.

• Black bears have good eyesight, and have been proven experimentally to be able to learn visual discrimination tasks based on color faster than chimpanzees and as fast as dogs.

• Black bears are strong swimmers, doing so to get from here to there and to feed (mostly on fish). They appear to enjoy swimming.

• Black bears may be active at any time of day or night, but mainly feed at night.

WEIGHT

• Adult males typically weigh 150–550 pounds, with 190-225 pounds a good average; females weigh up to 33% less at 120–150 pounds.

• All 16 black bear sub-species follow Bergmann's Rule – a principle that states that within a broadly distributed group of organisms believed to have evolved from a common ancestor – species of larger size are found in colder environments, and species of smaller size are found in warmer regions.

• The heaviest wild black bear ever recorded was a male from New Brunswick, shot in November 1972, that weighed 902 pounds after field dressing. Estimated live weight was 1,100 pounds. It measured 7.9 feet long. Another notable wild black bear, weighing 899 pounds in total, was the cattle-killer shot in 1921 on the Moqui Reservation in Arizona. The heaviest bear from New Jersey was shot in 2011 and weighed 830 pounds. A Pennsylvania bear taken in 2010 weighed 880 pounds.

There are extremes both larger and smaller. A friend killed a mature brown phase black bear in Ontario with a live weight of 135 pounds. The bear was aged at 16 years old. The bear I killed in Wisconsin in 2014 was in the mid-500 pound range and was only seven years old.

PREDATION

• As noted earlier, black bears do not prey much on large animals, but they will prey on deer fawns and elk fawns. They are known to follow pregnant does and cows, waiting for the fawn or calf to drop.

• In some northwestern areas they cause damage by stripping the bark from trees and feeding on the cambium.

• They can kill adult cattle and horses but prefer smaller domestic animals such as sheep, goats, calves and pigs. In colonial days, farmers let their hogs

What is the Black Bear?

run free in the woods in the warm months, letting them fatten on acorns in the fall. Bears loved this.

• Black bears scavenge only to a small degree. They prefer fresh foods. They don't particularly like fish, fresh or odorously old.

COAT

• The soft fur has dense underfur and long, coarse, thick guard hairs. Individual coat colors range from white, blonde, cinnamon, or light brown to dark chocolate brown or to jet black, with many intermediate variations. Two-tone colorations of a wide range of colors and locations on body, head and legs also occur.

• The white or cream kermode – the spirit bear -- exists in a small section of the central British Columbia coast. It is rare and protected. Glacier bears, occurring along parts of coastal Alaska, have a blue-toned coat.

• Many black bears in the northwest are cinnamon, blonde or light brown. Large individuals are sometimes mistaken for a grizzly bear.

• Some bears have a white "crescent moon" or irregularly shaped white spot on the chest.

Photo: Bill/Sandy Wiesner

• *Go west if you're looking for a color phase bear other than black. Eighty percent of the bears I saw on a Wyoming hunt were not black.*

SOUNDS / VOICE

• Bears communicate with each other through grunts, tongue-clicks and blowing. Momma bear usually communicates with us when we are on stand by clacking or 'popping' her teeth. This apparently is a sign of fear in the bear, but definitely a trigger for caution and extra alertness from the hunter in the tree. Biologists say "Bears that clack do not attack".

• The voice is resonant, not like a dog's growling or barking, and can be mimiced. Children and babies sound like cubs. Adult males may moan in fear or grumble when upset.

• When bears are nervous and/or crowded, they often stand their ground and bluff and bluster because they don't want to quit what they're doing but don't yet feel threatened enough to leave. If the bluster fails, they may jump forward, slap the ground or nearby vegetation, and a sort-of growl or blowing will occur. If nothing happens to make them more nervous, the bluster will subside. (Bluster is defined as 'forceful explosions of air accompanied by threatening body language and sometimes deeper, throaty snarls'.)

If you hear a bear huffing, usually when it is leaving a situation, the tension has eased.

• Bears also have sociable sounds among themselves. Mothers grunt when approaching cubs or calling them down from a tree; tongue-clicking is a sign of friendly contact, for play or mating; cubs make a hum when they nurse or are relaxed, like a cat purring.

A BEAR'S YEAR

Biologists identify five stages. The beginning and duration of each stage is genetically programmed to food availability in their region. When food is in short supply, they begin hibernating earlier. This could mean hibernating in September or October and not coming out of hibernation until April, and they may hibernate through winter thaws.

When mast crops and other fall foods are abundant, with some remaining available through the winter, bears generally don't begin hibernation until late November or December. They will hibernate less than five months, hibernation won't be as deep, and some individuals may come out to feed during a winter thaw. A very few will continue to feed through the winer when they find enough food.

THE FIVE STAGES
• Hibernation

Heart rate and metabolic rate decreases significantly. The bear's body uses huge amounts of stored energy per day, mainly body fat, as it sleeps. It breathes once every 45 seconds. Heart rate is reduced to less than 22 beats per minute. Blood flow to skeletal muscles can be reduced by 45 percent or more. The black bear is so biologically adapted to hibernation it does not eat, drink, urinate or defecate while hibernating. Pregnant females lose about 35 percent of their weight during hibernation; males and females without cubs lose about 30 percent of their weight.

Nitrogen waste from the bear's body is biochemically recycled back into their proteins. This prevents muscle loss, because the process uses waste products to build muscle during this long time of inactivity. In comparison to true hibernators, their body temperature does not drop significantly, staying around 95 degrees Fahrenheit.

Pregnant females make dens earlier than other bears, as early as late July in rare instances, and usually line their dens with more bedding than do non-pregnant females and males. Most females begin hibernation in mid September to mid October.

Males and non-pregnant females generally go into dens in mid November; farther south, out of snow country, they may not den until January.

• This bear must have had good food because it obviously had not yet denned for the winter. This was an early snow in high country.

Bears check out possible den sites all summer. If disturbed during winter, the bear will often move to another den.

They make a variety of beds, and they bed in a variety of places. Not all bears make beds if they den after snow has fallen, or they live in snow-less winter weather. If leaves raked together look like a bed, there will be a depression 2-4 feet in diameter. To check it, wet a palm and rub it in the leaves; black hairs will stick to your hand.

Den types are numerous: • caves and rock crevices; • holes dug into hillsides, under and among the roots of a tree; • under the crowns of fallen trees; • in brush piles; • or simply grass and leaves raked together on the downwind side of a thick windbreak. Bears like to den in hollow trees when they get the chance. There aren't many, unless there was a fire in the area years ago so tree cores have rotted.

Caves and holes in rock piles can be used for centuries, but an individual bear usually won't use this type of site in consecutive years. Secure dens are seldom used in consecutive years by one bear. Dug dens often collapse after use.

Tracks in mid-winter snow are usually made by a male bear that left its den, most likely during a warm spell. Males usually return to the den. Females normally do not leave the den.

Their footpads peel off during hibernation; tender tissue toughens in the spring as they move.

Bears leave the den in April in colder climates, but may leave in March in warmer climates.

In cold weather, especially in spring when the ground is still frozen, when they emerge from their den, they rake together leaf litter, and sometimes conifer tree boughs, to insulate themselves from the ground. If cedars are

What is the Black Bear?   11 available, they sometimes strip the bark for bedding.

They generally bed away from people and other bears, but there are plenty of verified instances of bedding under decks and porches in residential communities.

• Walking Hibernation

This is the two- to three-week period right after a bear comes out of the den, when its metabolism is adapting to summer levels. It eats and drinks less than it will in summer. It urinates less.

• Normal Activity

This usually lasts from green-up in the spring to the beginning of hyperphagia, which can begin in midsummer or fall. The bear eats well now -- 5,000-6,000 calories a day.

• Hyperphagia

This is the get-ready-for hibernation time. The bear eats and drinks heavily. If enough food is available, it will eat 15,000-20,000 calories a day and drink several gallons of water to help process that food and get rid of nitrogen-based waste. It will urinate two to four gallons daily

• Fall Transition

Now a bear's metabolism changes as it gets ready for hibernation. It eats less but drinks heavily to get rid of body wastes. It rests 22 hours or more a day. Its system begins to change. Active heart rate falls from 80-100 beats per minute to 50-60 beats per minute. Sleeping heart rate drops from 66-80 beats per minute to 22 beats per minute or slightly lower.

BREEDING & REPRODUCTION

• Mating is in late May or June, sometimes in early July. A male will roam great distances during the breeding season looking for a receptive female.

At a spring bear camp in Manitoba, one of the hunters shot at a bear quartering away and hit it too far forward, sending the arrow in behind the front shoulder to exit just inside the front of the same shoulder, not hitting any vital organs. We tracked the bear the following morning with the aid of a dog and did not find promising sign.

That night the same hunter was in a stand eight miles from the stand where he wounded the bear the previous afternoon. Late in the day, the same bear came to this stand, looking for a receptive female. This time the hunter's arrow flew true. The arrow still in the huge male's shoulder area confirmed it.

• Males and females are together only during breeding season. A female may mate with several males during her estrus. Cubs from the same litter may have different fathers.

• Females reproduce best when they weigh more than 175 pounds in the fall. They are in better physical condition at or above that weight.

• Once pregnant, females concentrate on getting fat to ensure healthier cubs and to have enough milk for them. If they do not become fat enough, they lose their cubs.

• Fertilized eggs do not implant on uterine walls immediately. Instead, they free-float in the uterus until November, about five months. When the eggs implant, they grow swiftly.

• Females breed at 2-1/2 years if they have had plenty of food, are in good condition and of a proper weight, giving birth at three years. First-litter age is more commonly 5-1/2 years. On the edges of black bear range where food is in short supply, females may not grow large enough to have successful pregnancies until they are 10-1/2 years old.

• Cubs are born in January, weighing eight ounces to one pound at birth, usually closer to one pound.

• The mother loses 3/8-2/3 pounds a day as her system converts fat, water and other body energy to milk.

• Cubs typically open their eyes after 28–40 days and begin walking after five weeks. At six weeks, they weigh 2-3 pounds. By early April, most cubs weigh 3-10 pounds, depending on the mother's weight and number of littermates competing for milk. At six months, cubs will weigh 40-60 pounds. They reach full growth at five years.

• Mother and cubs leave the den in early to mid April.

• Cubs are natural climbers, climbing from the time they leave the den.

• When they leave the den, the mother bear usually looks for a big tree, at the base of which she will rake a bed of leaves and/or needles (pines are favorite trees), and which the cubs can climb for security.

• As green-up begins, cubs and mother become more active, with the range of travel and feeding expanding as summer days pass. Mother and cubs enter the fall slowdown period together and hibernate together. They remain together after emergence until May, when the female bear is ready to mate again. The cubs will be yearlings.

• Often a male bear will attempt to kill the cubs in their first year so the female will come into heat and can be bred, thus shortening the standard two-year cycle by 50 percent.

Litter Size, Survival

• Most litters are two or three cubs. The record is six, in Pennsylvania. There usually will be three cubs when food is most abundant.

• Female bears that do not have enough food do not reproduce. They will breed, but the cubs will be absorbed 'in utero', be stillborn, or starve from lack of milk.

• Females usually have a litter every two years, but the frequency can be three or four years if the female does not get enough food.

• Litters of three cubs usually have the most surviving cubs. Litters of one or two cubs usually are from first-time mothers.

• It is estimated 60 percent of cubs survive past their first year. This will vary with food supply and condition of the mother bear as the two primary factors.

LONGEVITY

• In the wild, average lifespan is 15-18 years. The record age of a wild black bear is 31 years, in captivity it is 44 years.

Photo: Bill/Sandy Wiesner

• *Healthy, mature females tend to have three cubs every two years.*

What is the Black Bear?

CHAPTER 2 - Memoir
SPILLED ROTTEN FISH

After that wild beginning, the next several years found me at deer camp looking for another bear encounter. It was not to be, but I remained a hopeful kid.

Turn the clock ahead to 1966 -1969, my high school years. My teachers may not have believed it, but I learned a lot those years – mostly about deer hunting and black bears. I could hunt the north woods and use the high school library to learn more about the black bear.

In late 1969 I joined the Marine Corps, another family tradition. I saved as much money as I could because I had a plan in place well before my discharge in 1971.

My first purchase when I returned home was a brand new 1972 Ford F-150, all black, with a four-speed on the floor and a six-cylinder engine. I took it to my buddy's tire shop and put on custom rims and big tires. That poor six-cylinder had to work to turn those big tires, but I had the coolest looking bear hunting rig on the road.

Because there were no bears where I lived, I traveled to Beecher in northeastern Wisconsin to bait. My job at a manufacturing plant in Sturgeon Bay started at 7:00 am. I would drive two-and-a-half hours to my intended hunting area, bait the stands and drive back to Sturgeon Bay to clock in at work on time. Figuring five hours round trip on the road, and a couple of hours baiting, this meant getting out of bed at midnight.

The first three weeks of baiting, I made the trip three times a week. After that, it was every other day.

One Friday morning on my trip home I stopped at a roadside restaurant for a fast breakfast. An elderly gentleman, dressed in his outdoor attire, sipping on a cup of coffee, was the only other customer. I struck up a conversation and discovered he was a trapper.

My questions were many. I explained I was a bear hunter, trying to

Photo: Glenn Helgeland

• One of the biggest fallacies in bear hunting is that bears like odorous bait, and dead fish make the most odor. So, therefore, catch a bunch of suckers and let them decompose. Wrong, wrong, wrong. I tried this bait route once. Never again. Black bears like fresh bait, and they have a sweet tooth.

discover locations of bear in the area so I could bait and then hunt closer to home.

It seemed my existing baits were in good locations, but he asked what I used for bait. After explaining my 'secret' formula to him, he said he could give me the ultimate attractant. He asked if I could get my hands on some rough fish.

"I sure can," I said. "I live on Lake Michigan. It's too late this year, but in the spring suckers are plentiful."

" Here's what you do," he said. "Take a five gallon pail of suckers cut in chunks and set them out in the sun for the summer until you start baiting."

That's what I did.

During the summer, as the suckers decomposed, the odor that came from the pail was horrible. A wind off Lake Michigan gave us all a sample of the world's greatest bear attractant. I knew that it was offensive by the number, or lack of, visitors we had that summer. We couldn't escape that pail's aroma no matter where we set it, that's how powerful the stench was.

When baiting season came around, the contents of that pail had turned to liquid!

It was hard driving to the bait sites and back home with my secret scent in the bed of the truck. One morning I was travelling smooth, listening to tunes on the radio, sipping on a cup of coffee when a car pulled out from a side road right in front of me. I hit the brakes.

The sound I heard next was the five-gallon pail of my wonderful new attractant hitting the front of the truck box. In an instant that stench sent me bailing out of the truck. I emptied my stomach right there on the side of the road.

The trip home seemed like it would never end. The nice rubber mat I had in the back was headed to the dump. I tried everything but could not get the stink out of it. It was so bad, I doubt whether a dog would roll in it.

As the years passed, I often wondered if that old trapper had a good laugh over my greenhorn actions creating and handling what he said was the world's greatest bear attractant.

- - - - - -

• My 'secret' scent mixture ...

For an effective attractant scent, I boil sweet-smelling thimbleberries -- they grow in northern Wisconsin and bears love them -- with artificial honey and anise (available in the cooking supplies section of any grocery store) in a kettle on the stove. I turn the heat to low and stir often. When the mixture is a thick liquid it is ready.

I smear the mixture on trees around the bait. I never used drip cans or scent wicks in pre-season baiting. Once season opens, drip cans and scent wicks make sense because that will allow me to take them into and out of the bait scene as I want or need to.

The scent mixture and pre-season use has worked well. I use it to this day.

I pick wild thimbleberries because I like to and I know bears like them. Other berries should work, especially those grown wild or domestically in bear country.

The Black Bear's North American Range, Then and Now.

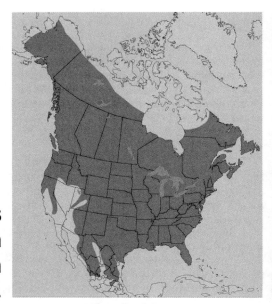

Historical Range

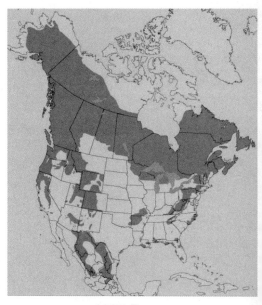

Maps courtesy of North American Bear Center, Ely, MN

1995 Range

• *The black bear has expanded its range a bit since 1995, and continues to expand it bit by bit. The black bear population in North America is healthy.*

CHAPTER 2 - How-To
DISTRIBUTION, POPULATION & RECORD BOOKS

DISTRIBUTION, TERRITORY & RANGE
The black bear is principally a forest animal but can be found from the far reaches of the north to the swamps of the south, Alaska to Florida and almost everywhere between. They also live in tundra areas of Alaska and Canada. In Labrador, where there are no other bear species, they live full-time on tundra. They live in more than 40 of the 50 states. For details, see the population estimates on the following page. Areas with large forests, swamps and ample food sources are ideal.

Today, they are primarily limited to sparsely settled, forested areas but are expanding their range into some farming regions and even to semi-residential areas.

The size of an individual bear's home range varies with the lack of or abundance of food. Yearling females often share territory with their mothers; young males may travel far to find their own territories. A mature female's home range may be just a few square miles. An adult male's breeding territory can cover more than 100 square miles, overlapping many female home ranges.

At highly productive food sources they may congregate and form dominance hierarchies, with the largest, most powerful males dominating the best feeding spots. (Bears that appear nervous at a bait are not the dominant bear feeding at that bait. The bear that walks in with no hesitation is the dominant one or the only one.)

Annual ranges held by mature male black bears have some variation. On Long Island off the coast of Washington, ranges average five square miles; on the Ungava Peninsula in Canada, ranges can average up to 1,000 square miles.

POPULATION ESTIMATES

This is a state-by-state and province-by-province estimate of black bear populations. These numbers are the estimates from surveys made by wildlife biologists and are as close as anyone can get to actual numbers.

State and federal agencies continually regulate bear numbers by setting harvest quotas. Some states issue a controlled number of permits, others control populations by closing the season once a total number of bears have been taken or a certain number of females have been taken.

Contact wildlife department offices from any state/province for information on seasons and number of permits available.

United States
- Alaska — 200,000
- Wisconsin — 35,000
- Washington — 30,000
- California — 30,000
- Oregon — 27,500
- Maine — 25,000
- Idaho — 20,000
- Minnesota — 20,000
- Michigan — 18,000
- Virginia — 16,000
- Pennsylvania — 14,000
- North Carolina — 13,000
- Colorado — 11,000
- Montana — 10,000
- West Virginia — 10,000
- New York — 6,500
- New Mexico — 6,000
- New Hampshire — 5,000
- Georgia — 5,000
- Tennessee — 4,500
- Vermont — 4,100
- Arkansas — 4,000
- New Jersey — 3,500
- Arizona — 3,000
- Massachusetts — 3,000
- Florida — 3,000
- Arizona — 3,000
- Utah — 2,000
- South Carolina — 1,200
- Oklahoma — 800
- Louisiana — 700
- Maryland — 600
- Connecticut — 350
- Texas — 250
- Nevada — 225
- Missouri — 200
- Mississippi — 180
- Ohio — 70
- Alabama — 50
- Rhode Island — 10
- Wyoming — Unknown

Estimated Total — 506,000

Canada
- Brit. Columbia — 140,000
- Ontario — 100,000
- Quebec — 70,000
- Alberta — 40,000
- Manitoba — 30,000
- Saskatchewan — 30,000
- New Brunswick — 16,000
- Yukon Territory — 10,000
- Newfoundland & Labrador — 8,000
- Nova Scotia — 7,000
- NW Territories — 5,000
- Prince Edward Is. — 0

(Black bears were extirpated from PEI in 1937.)

Estimated Total
400,000-456,000

COLORATION

The further west you travel, the higher the percentage of color phase bear you will see. On a Wyoming hunt, 80 percent of the bear seen and taken were color phase animals. This is the highest percentage of color phase bear I have encountered on an individual hunt.

My dream is to take a color phase bear. I have shot 57 black bears but no colored ones. In more than four decades of bear hunting I have seen only one colored bear. It was a cream color; unfortunately, it weighed only 75 pounds. On at least half a dozen occasions first-time bear hunters I was guiding took color phase bear. On an Ontario hunt some time ago, a German hunter in camp took a bear with four chocolate legs and head, with a cream colored body. Gorgeous bear! In camp, I overheard him telling the outfitter that black bear should be black. Can you believe that?

The editor/publisher of this book took a three-toned bear in northern Saskatchewan several years ago and a cinnamon in Ontario before that.

The states and provinces offering the best opportunity at a color-phase bear:

- Manitoba
- Saskatchewan
- Alberta
- British Columbia
- Wyoming
- Montana
- Colorado
- New Mexico
- Arizona
- California

• A Sample of Color Variations, By Location

- Michigan — 100% black
- Minnesota — 94% black, 6% brown
- New England — 100% black
- New York — 100% black
- Tennessee — 100% black
- Washington (coastal) — 99% black, 1% brown or blonde
- Washington (inland) — 21% black, 79% brown or blonde
- Yosemite Nat'l Park — 9% black, 91% brown or blonde

• RECORD BOOK ENTRIES

Entry totals from the Pope & Young Club and the Boone & Crockett Club, given below, can be a where-to-go guide if your goal is to take a color phase bear or a trophy-class bear.

For additional information, go to these websites:
- Pope & Young Club -- www.pope-young.org
- Boone & Crockett Club -- www.boone-crockett.org

Entry totals on following page.

POPE & YOUNG CLUB BLACK BEAR ENTRIES 1970-2015		BOONE & CROCKETT CLUB BLACK BEAR ENTRIES 1970-2015	

POPE & YOUNG CLUB
BLACK BEAR ENTRIES
1970-2015
(by state/province)
Minimum Score to Qualify:
• All Time -- 18
• No awards program separation

BOONE & CROCKETT CLUB
BLACK BEAR ENTRIES
1970-2015
(by state/province)
Minimum Score to Qualify:
• Awards Program – 20
• All Time – 21

Pope & Young		Boone & Crockett	
ONT	1,461	WI	594
SAS	980	PA	302
ALB	788	AK	223
MAN	706	SASK	220
WI	698	MN	165
AK	488	MAN	163
ID	420	CA	146
QUE	417	NC	125
MN	412	CO	123
C0	382	ALB	119
CA	248	AZ	116
BC	216	BC	111
ME	203	MI	106
MI	177	ONT	83
NBW	170	WA	68
NM	137	NY	56
MT	131	OR	53
WA	129	ID	47
NY	124	NM	46
OR	124	VA	45
WV	95	UT	43
UT	92	WY	42
AZ	88	ME	39
VA	69	QUE	36
AR	61	MT	28
WY	58	NFD	26
NH	44	NB	22
GA	25	AR	18
NFL	25	WV	18
NS	18	NJ	16
PA	15	VT	16
NC	14	GA	13
VT	13	NV	11
MA	11	MA	5
TN	6	NH	5
OK	5	FL	3
NWT	1	SC	3
YUK	1	OK	2
		MD	1
		TN	1

- Pope & Young offers an excellent opportunity to get a black bear trophy into the record book. Getting into Boone & Crockett is much more difficult.
- I found northern Ontario bears had the biggest skulls, all other things being equal.
- The number of hunters in any given state or province plays a big part in book entry totals. I'm sure more black bear hunters have, over the years, hunted Ontario. When you can get a tag, northern Wisconsin is tough to beat.

WHERE WOULD YOU GO TO TAKE A TROPHY BEAR?

What is your definition of a trophy bear? Are you looking for weight, skull measurement or size of the squared hide? Taking a big bear involves extra effort on your part when deciding where to hunt. Big bears are hard to locate and even harder to hunt. It is a matter of doing your homework prior to booking a hunt. If you plan to go with an outfitter, ask the number of big bear his clients have taken, and the size of those bear.

Photo: Bill Wiesner

Photo: Bill Wiesner

- *Nathan Ewing, an Illinois-based bear hunter, took this big color phase bear off a bait at the top of a Wyoming mountain reached by horseback. Eight bears were hitting the bait; all were a color phase other than black.*

- *Craig Harden took this immense male bear near Orr, Minnesota, off a bait enhanced with bear scent. Live weight was more than 800 pounds.*

Bottom line is simple -- put in the extra work required, separate yourself from everyone else just like big bears normally do among their kind, and do not be in a big hurry to hunt. Hunt only the best times and be cautious in every move.

• If you have deep pockets, Vancouver Island, British Columbia. Bears here typically are heavyweights and have huge heads. The island has a good population, so if you miss a chance at a trophy you could well have another opportunity. If you hunt an area that holds only one good bear, your chances are greatly reduced.

• Prince of Wales Island, Alaska. This hunt will be easier on the pocket book and has some monsters roaming the island. You can bait, call and spot-and-stalk there. The island also is noted for bears with large skulls, many over 20 inches. Check Alaska game laws to apply for a permit.

• Certain areas of Ontario have great bear. Go to northern Ontario for the bigger ones. My wife has arrowed two Boone and Crockett bears in Ontario.

• Manitoba, Saskatchewan and Alberta also have big bears, many of them color phase individuals.

• Wisconsin ranks near the top, too, in skull measurements and weights.

• Western bears have big heads but smaller bodies than Midwestern black bears and many of their northern counterparts. Ontario bears, too, tend to be big-headed and smaller-bodied in comparison.

Variations are due to genetics, food supply and age. I recall an area near Eagle Bay, Ontario, that had bear with larger than average skulls. It seemed that any male bear weighing 250 pounds or more had an 18-inch-or-larger skull. I hunted there three times and killed three Pope and Young bears. The heaviest bear was less than 300 pounds. On the other hand, I have shot bears 350 to 400 pounds that scored less than the 18-inch minimum.

In Wisconsin in 2013, my sons Brad and Bryan and I took three bears, two of which qualify for Boone and Crockett and one for Pope and Young.

Female bear skulls are usually much smaller than male skulls. A bear coming to your bait site that has a small head in proportion to its body size most likely will be a female.

A trophy bear isn't always the result of age. The average bear in the wild lives 15 to 18 years, but it may take 25 years or more for males to reach jumbo size.

MEASURING TERMS & STANDARDS

• Skull Measurement

P&Y/B&C records are based on skull measurement. This measurement is length of skull at its longest point plus width of skull at its widest point. Measurements are in sixteenths of an inch. Greatest length is measured between perpendiculars to the long axis of the skull without the lower jaw and excluding malformations. Greatest width is measured between the perpendiculars at right angles to the long axis.

Measuring instructions state, "All adhering flesh, membrane and cartilage must be completely removed before the drying period begins and official measurements are taken." Required drying time is 60 days.

Another item states, "If dogs are used, the hunter must be present at the time the dogs are released and no electronic collars can be used in pursuit."

• Weight

People always ask what the bear weighed. Anything over 500 pounds is really big. Although weight is not how bears are officially scored, with that in mind –

• The heaviest bear I have seen that was taken by an individual was a Minnesota giant that weighed more than 800 pounds.

• A 780-pound boar was taken in central Wisconsin in 2014. A bear illegally killed in 2008 weighed 720 pounds. In the early 1980's, Bob Faufau took a bear with a bow near Spirit Falls, Wisconsin, that weighed 777 pounds field dressed. In the bed of a three-quarter ton truck, its nose touched the front of the bed and its hind legs projected onto the tailgate. We talked with a guy who saw the bear. The largest bear recorded in Wisconsin was an 802-pounder killed in 1885.

• According to the North American Bear Center, the heaviest black bear reliably weighed – emphasis "reliably" -- was 880 pounds, taken in North Carolina in 1998. An 876-pound male was killed in Minnesota in 1994. An 856-pound bear was killed by a car near Winnipeg, Canada, in 2001.

• Squaring the Hide

In the West everything is in feet squared, as in "my bear squared 7' 1". When outfitters email trail camera photos to you to keep your blood boiling, they will tell you "this bear is a five-footer … that blonde one is a six-footer," etc.

There is no set rule to squaring a bear, but the most common method is to lay a skinned bear hide flat on a level surface, then measure the skin at its widest point (tip of front claws to tip of opposite front claws) and longest point (tip of nose to base of tail). Add the two numbers and divide by two. The result is the squared size.

There are variations, along the lines of "How big do you want it to be?" Sometimes the hide is measured with skull in, giving a bit of curvature and adding to the length measurement. Sometimes the hide is stretched lengthwise and measured, and then stretched paw to paw and measured. This creates the illusion of a much larger bear. In Alaska, this is known as the "peninsula stretch". Sometimes the hide is stretched in both directions at once, let relax, then laid flat and measured. Sometimes the hide is measured to the tip of the tail. Sometimes the width measurement is only to the tip of the paws, excluding the claws.

The biggest squared black bear I have seen was from northern Manitoba and squared just under eight feet. It was taken at a river bait.

An average male bear is 59" to 72" long; average female is 37" to 45" long. One of the largest bears recorded was 95 inches long and weighed more than 800 pounds.

Pope and Young Club Official Scoring System on following page.

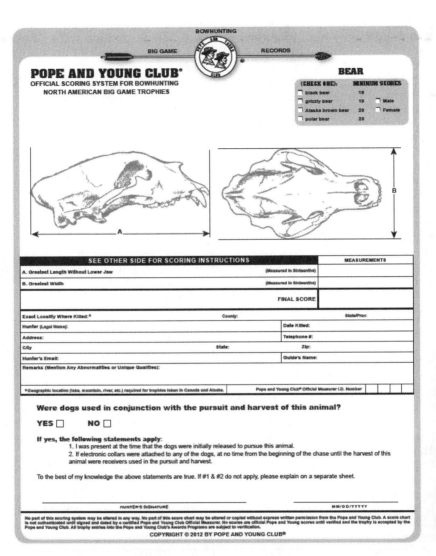

POPE AND YOUNG CLUB®

**OFFICIAL SCORING SYSTEM FOR BOWHUNTING
NORTH AMERICAN BIG GAME TROPHIES**

BEAR

(CHECK ONE):	MINIMUM SCORES
☐ black bear	18
☐ grizzly bear	19 ☐ Male
☐ Alaska brown bear	20 ☐ Female
☐ polar bear	20

SEE OTHER SIDE FOR SCORING INSTRUCTIONS		MEASUREMENTS
A. Greatest Length Without Lower Jaw	(Measured in Sixteenths)	
B. Greatest Width	(Measured in Sixteenths)	
	FINAL SCORE	

Exact Locality Where Killed:*	County:	State/Prov:

Hunter (Legal Name):	Date Killed:
Address:	Telephone #:
City	State:	Zip:
Hunter's Email:	Guide's Name:

Remarks (Mention Any Abnormalities or Unique Qualities):

*Geographic location (lake, mountain, river, etc.) required for trophies taken in Canada and Alaska.   Pope and Young Club® Official Measurer I.D. Number

Were dogs used in conjunction with the pursuit and harvest of this animal?

YES ☐   NO ☐

If yes, the following statements apply:
1. I was present at the time that the dogs were initially released to pursue this animal.
2. If electronic collars were attached to any of the dogs, at no time from the beginning of the chase until the harvest of this animal were receivers used in the pursuit and harvest.

To the best of my knowledge the above statements are true. If #1 & #2 do not apply, please explain on a separate sheet.

_____   _____
HUNTER'S SIGNATURE   MM/DD/YYYY

• *Scoresheet for bears, used by Pope & Young Club.*
Boone & Crockett Club measuring/scoring system is the same.

CHAPTER 3 - Memoir
MOST SATISFYING AND BIGGEST BEARS

MOST SATISFYING
When I owned Renegade bows, I often traveled to Dennis Patton's shop near Norway, Michigan, to talk about bow designs. Dennis had been the manufacturing boss at Bear Archery when it was in Grayling, Michigan. The conversation would always switch to Fred Bear. Fred was my bowhunting hero.

One day Dennis said he had something to show me.

He brought out a hard bow case. Inside the case was a set of recurve limbs and three magnesium risers. Back then it was far cheaper to make a riser than a set of laminated limbs. I believe it was a 62-inch bow; Fred had used it with a B-handle riser.

"Fred gave this bow to me several years ago," Dennis said. "Fred actually hunted with this bow, so it has that extra bit of in-the-field history."

"Hey, that bow's left-handed," were the first words out of my mouth. Of course. Fred shot left-handed. "I shoot left-handed."

I was drooling.

"I would love to shoot a bear with that bow," I said. His response nearly stunned me.

"Go for it," he said, and handed the bow to me.

I could not get home fast enough to shoot the bow. The top limb had a slight twist so I would shoot only three or four shots at a time to avoid twisting the limb further.

The next year, in 2001, I went to northern Saskatchewan on a spring bear hunt. I had been to this camp before, but this hunt was going to be special.

When I got there, with my Fred Bear bow carefully in tow, I was pretty wired, thinking about the next day's hunt with Fred Bear's bow. Sleep was out of the question, so I laid there in the dark and got even more wired.

Next day finally arrived, and my cameraman and I were soon sitting in

• *Fred Bear, my hero.*

• *The northern Saskatchewan bear I took shooting a bow that once belonged to Fred and with which Fred had hunted.*

our ground blind. Later that afternoon, while I alternated between watching out a blind window for a bear and then looking down at Fred's bow right there in my hands, a nice bear came into view and began approaching the bait

The bear passed within five feet of the ground blind as it moved to the bait. I shot it at less than 10 feet; double-lunged it good. The bear ran less than 20 yards. I watched it drop from the blind.

Oh man oh-man-ohman! I celebrated the life of Fred Bear that day and honored him in a way I will always remember. I would love to own that bow, but it is Dennis's bow. However, it thrills me to this day to think about that hunt and the fact that I shot a bear with Fred Bear's bow.

BIGGEST BEAR

In 2013, Brad, Bryan and I drew bear tags in Wisconsin. Bryan would be hound hunting in northwestern Wisconsin; Brad and I would be over baits in north central Wisconsin's Zone C, where no dogs can be used to hunt bear. Because of that, the season opens every year on the same weekend to bait sitters. Zones A, B and D allow hounds, so the opener rotates every year in those areas, with hound hunters having the first week one year and bait sitters the first week the next year.

My good friend and his family – Kurt and Carla Fischer, their daughter Sabrina and husband Ted Skarlueka, daughter Jessica and her husband Travis White – took care of the baits in the Antigo area for us and had bear coming in regularly. Bait materials were sweets, fryer grease and granola placed in a pre-positioned hollow stump.

Before baiting began, Kurt and I selected six bait sites on Ted's land. We needed only two, of course, but it's always good to have backups. I made the two-hour drive to Antigo as often as I could to help Kurt bait the stands

There were tracks of three adult bears at the bait where Brad planned to sit, and a sow with cubs on another bait. The bait site I would watch had a big bear track, just what you want to see.

This was a bait-and-blind set-up like nothing I'd seen. In fact, I thought it was the worst setup I'd ever seen. I was to sit on the edge of a creek, watching a bait hidden 75 yards away in tall grass on the other side of a plowed 15-acre field. To improve it, we (Kurt and I) had cleared a small shooting lane through the long grass to the bait stump. Any bear would offer a clear broadside shot as it stepped up to get a mouthful of bait.

Kurt wanted to try this bait site because Ted had seen bears there while working the field. It was nearly surrounded by swampy areas of long grass and willows. We found that the bear would lie in the long, wet grass to be cool.

Photos: Bill Wiesner

• *Bill's father, Bill Wiesner Sr., and his grandson Brad with a Wisconsin spring turkey the senior Wiesner shot.*

• *Bill and his largest black bear, a Wisconsin trophy that scored 21-15/16 and weighed 510 pounds. He shot it near the edge of a plowed field with what had been his father's .30-06.*

From scouting, we knew the bear would approach the bait site from the south through long grass on the west edge of the plowed field. The east side of the plowed field was the only place to sit that would give me good cover and an easy approach to the blind. My approach to the blind would be from the northeast, across the general prevailing wind direction.

I may have thought it wasn't much of a site, but that big track at the bait, a track that appeared more than once, indicated otherwise.

After two months of setting up stands and going to Antigo whenever possible to run baits, we were ready to hunt. Finally, opening day arrived and the hunt was on.

Bryan was using my .45/.70 guide gun to hunt with the hound men. He likes the rifle's shortness, so he can shoot quickly if the bear is in thick brush. Big bears do not like to tree; climbing is difficult for them. Dogs often bay a big bear, surrounding it on the ground, and the hunter may have to make a quick decision to shoot.

On the second day, Bryan shot a large bear in the morning, one that officially scored 22-4/16 inches. It weighed 500 pounds and was a trophy of a lifetime. Men and dogs jumped it off a bait early in the morning and ran it more than a mile through some thick, nasty swamp, with men and dogs and bear stopping now and then to catch their breath. Around 1 pm the bear bayed, still in the swamp. Bryan quickly found a clear shot at a good angle and the .45/70 spoke loudly and accurately. Hound men, dogs and Bryan were exhausted from the chase through the wet swamps.

Brad's stand was in a tree on the edge of a swamp. Two hours before dark a bear came into view on a trail leading to the bait. Brad could tell it wasn't the dominant bear hitting that bait but a shooter, nonetheless. The bear drifted off the trail and cautiously circled Brad's tree, with Brad trying to position himself for a shot as the bear moved. The bear remained in cover too heavy to allow a good shot, but after 10 nerve-wracking minutes, the bear moved into a position that gave Brad a clear shot with his .280 Ruger. The bear jumped, ran into the thick swamp, gave out one death moan – once you've heard it, you won't forget it – and expired. The bear was a 275-pound boar.

On the third evening of the hunt, I sat in the blind on the edge of the creek, watching the bait on the other side of the plowed field, with Kurt beside me ready to film the action. In my hands I held my dad's scoped .30-06 Remington pump deer rifle. I lost Dad in 2007 before I could take him on a bear hunt that I had promised him. My dad and I were close. He taught me all he could about the outdoors and his love for being in the outdoors, respect for animals, hunting and fishing, and I miss him every day.

At about 30 minutes before darkness, Kurt slipped out of his chair to get the truck, about a three-quarter-mile walk. He could get out of there without spooking the bear because he would be out of sight quickly by walking directly away from the bait and down a hill.

As I awaited darkness, with nothing happening, I decided to put the scope on the bait stump to see if I could still see enough through the scope to make a good shot in the low light. I put the crosshairs on the stump and suddenly a big black head came into clear view. That bear's appearance was so unexpected and so instantaneous, I almost dropped the rifle. I know my eyes opened quite a bit wider.

As the bear moved into shooting position, I aimed carefully, slipped off the safety and carefully squeezed the trigger. The bear dropped on the bait.

I hustled (as well as can be hustled across a plowed field by a person my size with poor wheels) to the bait. There lay a giant bear with a bucket of a head. The boar officially scored 21-15/16, short of Bryan's bear's score. After weighing both bears, we found mine was heavier by 10 pounds than his trophy bear.

You can talk hunting methods and ways to do things until you are blue in the face, but sometimes unusual settings and setups work. You never know until you try. This wasn't pure luck; this was created luck, where scouting and hunt preparation paid off.

An additional thrill and satisfaction came from the fact that I used Dad's rifle. While I sat and waited for a bear, I thought about Dad and his rifle, now mine, and of hunting with him and other thoughts a son will have about his father. I had hoped I could pass the torch with the rifle by using it to bag a bear, one he never got the chance to hunt for.

That I did, with one heck of a trophy. I believe he's happy.

CHAPTER 3 - How-To
HUNTING GEAR

This is not a nonsense question: What should be your goals in selecting a hunting arm to shoot a black bear?

1) Hit the lungs. Bears go down fastest, almost immediately, when hit there.

2) Two holes, an entry and an exit, to create a better blood trail.

3) Large holes, to bleed better, sooner.

4) Large enough caliber firearm and/or heavy enough draw weight bow to do the job.

The best way to reach these goals is by shooting adequate gear you can handle well, trust and are confident using. There is no silver bullet or silver broadhead, but there's more than one way to skin a cat.

Consider the hunting arm you choose: • Rifle • Shotgun • Pistol • Muzzleloader • Bow • Crossbow.

FIREARMS

RIFLES

There are dozens of good cartridge options to choose from. Any good, flat shooting deer rifle, from a .270 up to and beyond a .375 H&H Magnum, will do the job. Bullet placement is key, of course, so use a rifle you are comfortable with and can shoot consistently and accurately without flinching. Those factors are more important than the amount of kinetic energy it produces.

You want the ability to anchor a bear at close range or reach out and touch one at longer distances, and you want to be able to see the target clearly so you can identify an exact aiming point. You should not shoot at a black blob, but too many firearms hunters do. Because of that, it is no surprise to hear outfitters say bear hunters using firearms wound and lose more bears than do bowhunters.

An adjustable-power scope (2x-7x, 3x-9x) will cover your needs at short and long ranges. If you will have short-range shots only, a 1x-3x scope would be fine. No matter what you use, be sure the scope has thick enough crosshairs that can be seen clearly in low light conditions, such as when black bear emerges from dark brush cover in the last few minutes of the day hunting hours.

BULLETS

Use any bullet that's designed to expand rapidly. A heavy-for-caliber bullet works well because that style tends to be longer with higher sectional density that generally penetrates deeper.

Over the last 10 to 20 years, bullet design has advanced dramatically and there really aren't any "bad" bullets out there, but there are some really good ones for specific requirements. A serious consideration for a bear bullet is more than just what it will take to kill the bear. Bears are known for NOT leaving a good blood trail. You want a bullet that punches a big hole preferably on both sides of the bear. There are many "premium" bullets now with a tip that expands rapidly but also have a heavily constructed body that holds together to penetrate deeply. Swift A Frames, Nosler Partitions, Bear Claws and Barnes bullets are good examples.

SHOTGUNS

Twenty-gauge, 16-gauge, 12-gauge – they all get the job done. The 12-gauge ranks at the top mainly because of slug weight. There are a variety of slugs available, from the standard rifled slug to the more recent saboted slugs. The big, heavy bullet creates substantial holes, creating a better chance for a good blood trail.

Shotguns are excellent for the close-in shooting you get when hunting with dogs, or over bait. A shotgun comes up fast when needed, and with short slug barrel (18"-20") it is a great choice for bear.

A 1x-3x scope is fine here.

HANDGUNS

You want a cartridge that will do the job well -- .44 Mag., .375 Mag. .41 Mag, .45 Colt and .454 Casull – are effective. Shooting a .454 Casull is not an enjoyable experience. All it lacks are wheels to be a small cannon. It best suited for people with large frames and strong wrists. For anyone else it is tough to shoot accurately.

Single-action revolvers have to be cocked to shoot by physically pulling the hammer back. This is a simple action that will rarely let you down. The longer-barreled (7-1/2" to 9'), more accurate revolver, when outfitted with scope, is an effective, reliable hunting arm.

Single-shot revolvers are great for the variety of calibers available.

Double-actions have a long pull (to cock the hammer) that makes them very hard to shoot accurately, although some double actions can be manually cocked and shot as single actions.

My personal handgun is a single-action revolver. It forces me to take my time with each shot, and it has a clean trigger pull.

A front-of-chest holster works well because the handgun can be drawn with minimal movement.

Open sights, handgun scopes and red-dot sights are available. I have shot a lot of handguns (qualified top in my battalion in the Marine Corps), and from that level of experience, I have no trouble saying scopes are not to my liking. However, they may be to yours. To help me with open sights, I carry a good range finder that is easy to get at and to use.

Shooting is a two-handed job requiring plenty of practice. Little shooting is offhand, for obvious reasons. You'll want a solid rest, such as a tree or a shooting stick.

Keep in mind that you cannot take a handgun into Canada.

MUZZLELOADERS

The bottom line here is the bullet and amount of propellant. Whether it's an in-line, percussion cap or even a flintlock makes no difference as to its effectiveness. It's like shooting a .30-30 shell from a semi-auto rifle, a lever action or a bolt action - the bullet performance is the same. In-lines lend themselves much better to mounting scopes, have the fastest lock times and are most dependable. They probably represent more than 95 percent of the muzzleloading market today.

Rifles of .50 caliber are a huge percentage of the current market and would be the minimum with heavier bullets (275-350 grains) but for round balls you might be better off with a .54 caliber or .58 caliber, based mainly on the weight of the bullet. A .50 caliber lead ball weighs only 178 grains.

Barrel length with muzzleloaders is a serious consideration, because longer barrels equal more velocity but are unwieldy, so a compromise, usually 26 inches to 28 inches, is most common.

As for powders, be aware that Pyrodex pellets come in 30 grains and 50 grains, so always think in total grains for a load instead of number of pellets. Using three 50-grain pellets in many muzzleloaders is considered unsafe. Black powder is still the standard by weight, but it is more volatile and dirty to shoot, so almost everyone is using black powder substitutes like Pyrodex and several others. The tricky part is that they don't equate exactly to black powder by weight, so there is some "working up" needed in most cases. Around 90 to 100 grains usually provide the best combination of velocity and accuracy in a .50 caliber muzzleloader, which is three 30-grain or two 50-gain pellets.

The technology is changing. Some muzzleloaders now can take three 50-grain pellets; the new Remington can take even more. Pellets are more convenient, but in most cases loose powder (black powder, Pyrodex, Triple 7 and others) is more efficient and consistent.

Pellets, and some styles of muzzleloading rifles and types of sights, are not legal for use in some muzzleloading seasons.

ARCHERY

• BOW

Your deer hunting equipment will work just fine. Bottom line, of course, is to use the combination of bow style and draw weight, sight, arrow weight and length, and broadhead, that works best for you and with which you feel completely confident. That will clear your mind and let you focus on the shot. As with hunting deer, some hunters prefer light arrows and light broadheads for faster, flatter shots. Other hunters want heavier draw weight, heavier arrow weight and heavier broadeads for better penetration. Two holes bleed better than one.

Bears can be killed with bows in the 45-pound draw weight range, or even slightly less. (Be sure the draw weight meets state or province law.) At that draw weight you really have to pick the spot to shoot through the bear's body to get two holes. Using a ground blind would be good, so you can aim at the lower half of the bear's vitals. There is less bone protection. You would have a better chance of a pass-through arrow and thus a better chance for a quickly-effective hit and better blood trail.

Many bow hunters overbow themselves for bear. A bear is a soft-tissued animal and can easily be taken with your deer set-up. My wife and daughter-in-law use 45-pound draw weight bows and have had no problems. They also are darned good shots.

Recurves and longbows are great black bear bows. Most shots should be only 10-15 yards. Choose your equipment and allow yourself plenty of time for practice.

Mechanical broadheads will work fine on vertical bows that produce enough speed and kinetic energy. Low poundage bows in the 50 pounds and under range do not fit well with mechanical broadheads because they do not have the needed energy to make the mechanical heads perform as intended.

• CROSSBOW

Some crossbows are bore-sighted at the factory and are equipped with scopes. The typical crossbow scope is either 3x or 4x magnification power, many with multiple crosshairs and/or dots. Once sighted in, they are accurate out to 20, 30 and 40 yards or more. Practice at various distances to learn how your arrow set-up will perform with broadheads. If you need to make adjustments, do so before going into the woods to hunt.

Mechanical broadheads generally work well out of crossbows, but you must pay attention to the speed of your crossbow. For crossbows over 350 feet-per-second, you must use mechanical broadheads that are specifically designed to prevent them from opening prematurely in flight.

A shooting stick is an invaluable tool for crossbow users. Many youth, women, seniors and physically challenged individuals are not able to support the weight of the crossbow without assistance.

One thought on crossbows: spot-and-stalk isn't a good setting for their use. Their horizontal nature can be more difficult to keep hidden; they can be heavy and difficult/tiring to carry; they never should be carried cocked cocking creates considerable movement (and possibly noise, too) that could easily spook a bear, and, once cocked, they can be unsafe to move with.

Crossbows have their place, and they are good for youth and hunters unable or unwilling to shoot a vertical bow, but that place is far better in a treestand or ground blind and, under certain controlled conditions, when hunting with dogs or on a guided hunt.

PRACTICING

Know your effective distances and practice shooting at a 3-D target from different angles and distances. Always practice shooting quickly; bears sometimes do not offer much of a time window in which to get the shot off. If you are using a bow, try to draw early enough prior to the shot and follow the bear. When you are at full draw and anchored, you have a much better chance at making a killing shot.

If drawing that early isn't practical, draw and shoot at the first good opportunity. That could be at the bait after the bear has relaxed and is focused on what it is eating. Above all, do not rush the shot.

Photos: Bill/Sandy Wiesner

• *For hunting with hounds, practice shooting at a target in a tree, such as Sandy is doing here. The target is a Rinehart 3-D Anatomy Bear.*

EVERYTHING ELSE

CASES

Protect your gear from dirt and shock. A strong, hard case will protect gear when traveling to hunting camp or on a four-wheeler to your stand. You may encounter mud, water, rocks, glancing blows off trees, or all of these and more. Open back-country roads can be dusty; dust isn't good for scopes, sight settings, compound bow wheels, etc. Bouncing on a rough road or two-track can affect scope and bowsight settings. Check them frequently. Shoot a couple of times in camp to check.

TREESTANDS

Portable stands with climbing sticks work well in the bear hunting woods; most trees are evergreens and a portable stand can be hung to best suit your shooting needs -- left or right handed, best tree for a good shot from stand to bait. A portable stand and climbing sticks are easy to carry into the thick bear woods. Be sure to check the stand's weight rating if you're a big guy.

Ladder stands are the safest and easiest to set up, easiest to climb into and get out of, and offer the best security. Check all joints; they can squeak when you shift weight. Vegetable oil on the noisy joints normally quiets them. Take a board with you to put under the ladder so the legs will be level and won't sink into the ground.

Climbing stands do not work well in bear woods because conifers predominate and are the best stand trees. They hide you so well.

You probably will encounter permanent stands on guided hunts. Be sure you climb into the stand in the daylight to check the stand – solid support and platform boards, solid and secure steps, secure platform solidly nailed to supports, permanent seats secure. Best permanent stand I've seen was fastened between two spruce trees, with a permanent seat at both ends, ready for left-handers and right-handers.

For stand preparation, a hand pruner, longer-handled branch pruner and folding saw will take care of everything you'll need to cut or trim.

• Small and large hand pruners and a folding saw are essential for trimming at a treestand, blind and bait site.

Photo: Glenn Helgeland

GROUND BLIND

Be sure the ground blind is large enough, in width and height, for gun and bow clearance, and of solid fabric, not plastic. Window covers should have silent hooks, not velcro.

The carrying bag should have a shoulder strap for easy carrying.

CHAIR / STOOL

Must be silent when you swivel on the seat, have big feet so it sits flat on ground and doesn't tip, and be comfortable for long sits. Best to have a back to lean against.

CLOTHING

First, check bear hunting regulations in the state or province you plan to hunt. Regulations can and do differ. Two examples:

• Saskatchewan law – rifle hunters must wear a vest of white, orange or red, and a hat of orange or red; bowhunters and muzzleloader hunters may wear camo.

• Wisconsin law – If you're hunting bear during the two-day youth gun deer hunt in October, at least 50 percent of your outer clothing above the waist must be blaze orange.

Camouflage is permissible most of the time in most of the places, but check the regulations.

No matter where you hunt, all clothing must be quiet, of course, so you can move without noise. Your deer hunting camo should work fine. Base layers should include a couple of long sleeved turtlenecks to help with insect control. Don't wear cotton; it holds moisture and will chill you if you perspire getting to your stand.

Rain gear must be quiet, too. To be sure that it is, put a soft outer garment over it.

That one mosquito that sneaks inside your head net and drives you to distraction? Main defense is to rub repellent on your face, forehead and neck. It will still get in, but you can keep it at bay. Or use a Thermacell rig.

Use gray duct tape to tape pants cuffs to boots as insect control, or stuff your pants cuffs inside knee-high boots. Wear a couple pairs of fairly loose pants as defense against mosquitos; if your pants constrict when you sit down, expect trouble. Mosquito stingers can easily go through one layer of pants, especially when the pants are tight against your skin.

Wear a jones-style hat (1-1/4 inch brim all the way around) so the brim keeps your head net away from your skin. If the net touches your nose, blackflies will cut the tip of your nose so much the blood from their bites will seal the net to the tip of your nose as it coagulates, but you won't be aware of it. Ripping that head net from your nose is not pleasant. The publisher speaks from personal experience.

If mosquitos are numerous and active, you will have to learn to ignore the incessant humming. A swampful of flying mosquitos produces a sound much like a slow-moving freight train in the distance, hour after hour after....

Gloves – Latex for baiting and regular camo for wearing on stand. Take a couple pairs of regular camo gloves, should one get rained on and need to dry, or get covered by pine pitch on stand. Pitch sticks to everything.

Camouflage

Contrary to popular belief, a black bear's eyesight is good. They catch movement fairly well, so move slowly when you must move. Or be in position to do nothing other than lift gun or bow.

This is not critical, but try to wear camo patterns that blend with the colors and light/dark tones of the location you are hunting. Actually, light/dark tones are more important than color as an effective element of camouflage. Swamps and thick conifers generally call for dark camo. Green and black checked flannel or wool shirts and jackets work well, too.

Ghillie or leafy suits allow you to set up anywhere.

Realize that your hands, arms and head move the most when you're on stand. Break your outline and be as motionless as possible.

FOOTWEAR

Take comfortable boots to hunt in and rubber knee boots or hip boots possibly for getting to your stand and definitely for tracking/trailing. Wounded bears go to wet and nasty areas when shot. Have comfortable camp shoes, too.

Photo: Glenn Helgeland

• *To keep mosquitoes at bay, tape your pants cuff or tuck one pair inside a long sock and the outer cuffs inside knee boots. Take comfortable boots to hunt in and rubber knee boots for wet walking/trailing conditions.*

SAFETY HARNESS

Definitely use one. Be sure you can move, stand up, look behind your tree without restriction from the belt, and that you can shoot from different positions without the harness obstructing movement or getting in the way of bow or gun.

SCENT CONTROL

Wear rubber or latex gloves when handling bait or scent attractants. Shower with scent-free soap or baking soda.   Store clothes in air-tight containers with small heavily-needled or leafed branches from trees in the area you hunt.   Dress in hunting gear when you park your truck or are dropped off. Spray yourself head to foot with scent-free spray right before you begin your approach to the bait. Always, of course, and most important -- play the wind.

INSECT REPELLENT

Standard insect repellent (spray or rub-on) works well and has been around forever. On a guided hunt, use the same repellent the outfitter uses, so there's a consistent aroma at the bait.

Rub the repellent on your skin so you know you have full coverage. Spraying repellent on your skin doesn't do the job. The spray, and active mosquito-repelling ingredients, come to rest on arm hairs or rest too lightly on bare skin.   When the carrying agent evaporates, you're poorly protected.

After repellent application, tuck your head net inside your turtleneck.

Thermacell is a good repellent for all insects.   Place a drop or two of anise oil on the pad before igniting it; the unit will spread the anise scent and keep insects away. Bears love the smell of anise.

PEPPER SPRAY

Weaker pepper sprays have proven adequate against black bears. With some sprays, aim at the bear's eyes. With sprays that shoot a mist, just aim at the bear's head. Don't put sprays on gear or blinds or tents. For some reason bears like to roll on pepper scented items. The law allows capsaicin content up to two percent. Commercial airlines do not allow most sprays to be taken onboard.

CHAPTER 4 - Memoir
LIVING IN THE BOONDOCKS

After the shipyard closed in Ontonagon in late 1981, Sandy, the boys and I moved from White Pine, Michigan, to a small three-room log cabin in the middle of nowhere. We were five miles south of Lake Superior on a gravel road dead center of Michigan's Upper Peninsula, the UP.

When the yard closed, our friend Gary Monville offered the cabin to us if I agreed to work bear bait sites for his hunting clients several miles south of my baits and the cabin. He had built the cabin for himself and his wife, but she didn't like the insects that live in cabins and in the woods (mostly the woods, fortunately) so they stayed in White Pine. We had two options – to remain in the UP and try to establish a guiding service or to move back to Wisconsin. Licenses could be purchased over the counter at that time and bears were plentiful, so we stayed. I started BEARCRAZY BILL'S GUIDE SERVICE for bear hunters. Turned out to be some of the best days of my life.

Baiting began the week of the fourth of July, baiting every other day until August 15 and every day from August 15 until September 10, when season opened. We had 25 bait sites, some a mile off the road. We walked to every one of them. I carried a trapper's pack full of goodies on my back. All four of us would leave the cabin at first light. These were all-day baiting sessions. We got in great physical shape over the summer.

Bait was stored in a friend's homemade trailer that had been converted to a freezer. It held all the bait we needed. Our bait was brought up from bakeries in Sturgeon Bay. Bait was easy to get because no one else collected bear bait in Sturgeon Bay. We had sweets of all kinds, bread, used fryer grease, meat scraps (legal in Michigan). We put out five gallons of bait every time we baited a stand, so with 25 bait sites we put out 125 gallons of bait on every run.

My goal was to do everything possible to be sure every client Gary had and every client I had, 15 to 20 hunters over three or four weeks of hunting,

• *I started BearCrazy Bill's Guide Service for clients and friends. We put five pounds of bait at each site; with 25 sites, that meant 125 pounds of bait every day as season neared.*

got a good shot opportunity, not just a shot opportunity. Our kill rate was 75 to 80 percent.

Our only concern living at the cabin was that there were no phones. Brad was nine and Bryan six. School was 20 miles away in White Pine; we had to take them and pick them up every day.

Our goal was to live in the outdoors with no one to answer to, to live simply and live off the land as much as possible and practical. It was an opportunity to teach kids about the outdoors. We had personal alone times and family alone times.

It was an opportunity for me to continue studying bears on a full-time basis, my life's passion. I also was big into being conservative and living off the land.

Sandy liked being able to pick berries and make jam. She wanted to hone her hunting and woods skills (learning animal tracks, runways, rubs made by deer and bear, and other animal sign); spending time with me and the boys, and preparing wild game. Although she already was good, she got better.

Brad and Bryan helped with the cutting, hauling and stacking of wood, the only heat source we had; picking berries to help Sandy make jam; learning to shoot bows, guns and slingshots, and carrying pails of bait to bait sites (competing to see who could carry their pails the farthest). They would collect wood ticks and stick them on their chest until we got back to the cabin, then put the ticks one at a time into an ash tray and pop them with lighted matches. They were most excited by baiting bears, swimming in the pond across the road, and catching panfish from the small local lakes.

It was incredible how much Mother Nature taught all of us about the outdoors, not only about bears but also the woods and everything it had to offer.

Every creature can teach us about life cycles. We often listened to songbirds and tried to mimic their vocalizations. We would watch and listen to the cadence of small game as they moved, then try to mimic the way they moved, in an attempt not to sound like a human. We listened to deer and bear vocalizations to try to determine what they were saying.

40   Living in the Boondocks

We fished panfish from shore and enjoyed great meals as a result. Our favorite, though, was to stretch a long string with dropper lines about a foot apart, baiting the dropper lines with small pieces of sucker meat, then hanging the line across the shallows of streams just before dark. Pulled at first light the next morning, each of the dropper lines would have a crayfish clinging tightly to the sucker meat. We boiled them like lobsters. Delicious!

Other natural foods were great. In the spring we picked fiddlehead ferns, cutting each stem close to the ground. They grow in bunches. We cut each bunch into pieces about the size of a quarter and boiled them in salted water until tender. Then we ate them, seasoned with butter, salt and pepper. Delicious!

There were also the ever-delicious morel mushrooms. Wild onions were everywhere; they made great eating and once in your system would keep mosquitoes, black flies and wood ticks away. Sure, you smelled like onion, but so what. Where we were living it didn't matter. Berries were abundant -- blackberries, wild strawberries, raspberries and thimbleberries. We ate like kings and ate healthy.

It was paradise for us. The absence of neighbors was of no concern. We had our family, and that was all we wished for. I liked the opportunity to be alone now and then; it was a good counter to having been in the Marines even though that was 10 years in the past. Friends stopped in occasionally, usually about the time Sandy's cooking was ready to put on the table. We were always busy, and we seemed to be doing something all the time. The family time was fulfilling. On rainy days we each would sit on a corner of a bed and play catch with a set mouse trap. If you sprung the trap when catching or throwing it, you were out. The winner didn't spring the trap, of course.

Photos: Glenn Helgeland

• **We ate nature's finest – morel mushrooms, wild strawberries and many more berries that Sandy made into jam.**

Problems? More issues than problems: lengthy power outages, lasting up to three days, which we worked around with lanterns and a Coleman stove; doctors and a hospital 25 miles away and the related concern of getting to either in the winter through deep snow.

We lived there two-and-a-quarter wonderful years.

Moving away was the most difficult decision we have ever made. We felt as the boys got older they needed more communication with other people. They both were going to be good in sports, and back home the programs were much better. I had a great job offer at a shipyard in Sturgeon Bay. We moved back, but not without bumps in the daily road. The boys were upset with Sandy and me; they loved what they had at that cabin and surroundings in the UP. Sandy and I were heartbroken the day we left. We still can't drive by that cabin when we visit the UP.

CHAPTER 4 - How-To
HUNTING STYLES

THE KEY TO HUNTING SUCCESS

Pre-hunt preparation is paramount! I have found over the years that the better prepared I was for a hunt, the more successful I was.

You must make the same thorough preparation -- physically, mentally, shooting competence, the proper and necessary gear – for each style of hunting you will be doing.

• If you are going on a **paid hunt, your guide** can do only as much as you allow him to do. If you cannot do what he needs you to do, all is lost. Make sure to communicate with him often before you leave on your hunt and do not be afraid to ask questions.

• If you will be **hunting with hounds and hound men**, ask about procedures, the do's and don'ts for your safety and improved chances of success. The outfitters and hounds know what is taking place, but you may not. You must be a help, not a hindrance; at the very least, know how and when to stay out of the way, when to follow, and when to do exactly what your guide tells you to do. In the heat of the chase it is too late to be asking questions.

• If you are **hunting on your own**, weigh all considerations. Will you have the time to bait properly and at the right time of day? Have you found a place to hunt that will best suit your baiting needs? Do you have the overall time and budget to make it a good hunt?

Be prepared. Insure your enjoyment of the bear hunt.

LEARNING PROGRESSION

Learning the complete methods of bear hunting is a task that will never be finished. This will always be an enjoyable work in progress. The black bear is such an amazing animal that anyone trying to learn its habits, life characteristics and behavior must be prepared to spend great amounts of time studying it.

Bears will do things that totally destroy some of your prior beliefs. They have their own agenda and will change it for no obvious (to us) reason. After more than four decades in the bear woods, I have learned one thing: I will not live long enough to totally understand the black bear, and I am fine with that.

* * * * * * * * * *
DO-IT-YOURSELF HUNT

This is a roadmap to help you reach your goal of the ultimate experience in bear hunting and have a good time doing so.

For D-I-Y, there are three important words to remember – preparation, preparation, preparation. This is ultra-vital on a D-I-Y bear hunt because a D-I-Y effort encompasses every detail from beginning planning to taking care of meat and hide of the bears you and hunting partners tag.

Your are your own outfitter, guide, and hide and meat processor. And you intend to have time to hunt, too? Because you are on your own, you need to be more organized and prepared to pay closer attention to detail.

Make a written list of questions, and make notes as needed when you talk to the various people you will need to talk to. Write down everything.

A categorized supply list is great for checking everything you need to bring -- hunting gear, shooting gear, clothing, baiting supplies, camping gear, food and cooking gear, bear processing tools. With a detailed list, you can track things more closely and minimize anxiety.

Planning, analyzing and preparation will be a continuous juggling game of decisions. Be prepared to shift gears and adapt options as you wade through the details. Don't expect to have all the answers right away.

CHECKLIST and QUESTIONS

This step-by-step planning / preparation list is as complete as we could make it. We may have overlooked something, but not much. Other chapters in this book will directly help you with planning details.
- **Planning the Hunt**
  - What is your budget?
  - How much time do you have available, portal to portal?
  - What type of hunt do you want?
  - Where, geographically, do you want to hunt?
  - Do you want to hunt spring or fall?
  - Are you the boss, or is this a committee thing?
  - How many people will be in your hunting party? (To know amounts of various items to bring.)
  - What is their bear hunting experience? (How much will they be able to help?)
  - **Other 'Musts'**
  - Know all applicable laws where you intend to hunt. If you're not a Canadian citizen and have a no-no or two in your history, you may not be able to hunt in Canada.
  - Get a passport if you don't have one. U.S. citizens cannot enter Canada without a valid passport.

CATEGORIES / GROUPS

• **Vehicle** – Condition, grease/oil before leaving, spare tire(s), adequate jacks, something to put jack on so it won't sink in mud when you need to change a flat back in the brush on a two-track trail, chain to pull you out of mud. Second vehicle to help first vehicle, or winch on first vehicle.

Photo: Bill/Sandy Wiesner

• *ATVs save time and work on all hunts, but especially on D-I-Y hunts where you have to do everything, including bringing out a bear. Some baits can be an hour or more back in the woods off a road.*

• **Lodging** -- Where will you stay, en route and at your hunt site? Motel, resort cabin, your tent or trailer at resort or campground? Will campground permit a hunting camp and all it entails on its grounds? Thinking here mostly of bait storage, processing of tagged bear, etc.

• **Camp needs** – Food, beverages, coolers for food and bait, stove(s) and suitable gas (LP or white), pots & pans, table(s), cooking and eating utensils, plates-dishes-cups, kitchen supplies (soap, scrub brush, towels, dish rack), matches.

• **Meat and hide handling supplies** -- Knives-sharpeners-steels, coolers for bait and ice (bagged regular ice and/or dry ice), salt for bear hide, meat packing bags.

• **Hunting gear** -- What hunting arm(s) do you intend to use? (May have an opportunity to use more than one type, but no handguns in Canada.) Shovel, axe, hatchet, rake, saw, five-gallon pail(s), attractant and masking scents and lures, gun/bow case and tools, treestand, treesteps, ground blind(s).

• COST OF THE HUNT
  • Travel (fuel and food) and lodging to and from your hunting site
  • Camp or resort cost
  • Food in camp
  • Price of fuel where you will hunt
  • License
  • Bait
  • Processing and transportation items to handle bear hide and meat properly, including ice/dry ice and salt.
  • Plan B if costs of the hunt you want may not fit your budget or number of days available are too few or distance to be travelled is too far for the time available.

• TYPE OF D-I-Y HUNT
  Spot-and-stalk? Calling? Bait hunting? Combination?

This decision will be influenced by several factors:
- The area you want to hunt may not be suitable for the type of hunt you want;
- The time available may not be enough to allow travel time and enough hunting days;
- The season may not be right for what you want to do;
- Don't try to do too much.

Personal gear:
- Insect repellent
- Duct tape
- Personal toiletries (tooth brush, etc.)
- Skin care medication (treat poison ivy, wild parsnip)
- Soap, washcloth, towel
- Medications. Always bring extra, should your stay be extended.
- Rain suit
- Extra pair of glasses, if you wear them
- Camo clothes, hat, gloves
- Gun - extra rounds of ammunition
- Bow - practice target and extra arrows

ADVANCE CAREFULLY

Once you know your time frame and budget, the next question is "which becomes the chicken and which the egg – where you want to hunt or how you want to hunt?"

Costs and time available will have a larger affect on where you hunt than how you intend to hunt. Some of this is academic because no one is going to launch a safari the first time he tries a D-I-Y hunt.

You most likely already have a hunt location and hunting style in mind before you decide to try a D-I-Y. **If you've been on a couple of guided hunts – a good way to get your feet wet before trying a D-I-Y – you're already well into the process.**
- Spot-and-stalk works best in the spring or early fall.
- Calling works well in the spring breeding season.
- Bait hunting requires more attention and far more effort, but most likely will be more productive. You have to collect, transport and store bait. In this, use manageable, sealable containers, ones that you can handle easily and which can be transported easily in truck, van or trailer. You do NOT want to haul 55- gallon drums. Do not use bait that will spoil -- meat, fish, etc. Bears don't like spoiled foods.

To hunt in Canada over bait, be aware that all bait brought into Canada has to be edible – by humans. Well…at least you'll know what to do when you get hungry on stand.

• WHERE TO STAY

If you plan to stay in a resort cabin, be sure you know what is included and what is not. Do you need to bring towels and bedding? Who does the clean-up, you or the resort's housekeeping staff? Can you cook in the cabin/ motel, or outside on the grounds? Do you need to bring food or are there stores in the area?

If you're thinking campground on public lands, what's allowed and what isn't?

How far will it be from your camp to where you plan to hunt (time and fuel cost factors)?

MEAT AND HIDE CARE

Are meat lockers or freezer facilities available in the area to cool your bear? (In Canada, ask about an abattoir, not a meat market or butcher shop.)
Go to Chapter 9 – Meat and Hide Care – for details.

• HUNT GEAR & BEAR-HANDLING ITEMS

- Pack frame
- Compass or GPS
- Rope, 3/8" - 30 feet, at least
- Hydrogen peroxide. Spray on anything you think is blood; If it is blood it will foam.
- Knee boots, probably hip boots, too. Although you may be able to walk into your stand without getting wet feet, a wounded bear will head to water if possible.
- Sharp knife(s), sharpening steel and stone
- Flashlights and extra batteries
- Camp lanterns, maybe, and white gas fuel
- Machete to cut brush
- Backup gun. Usually a shotgun, buckshot and slugs
- Ziploc bags (fish fillets, etc.)

- Tag for the bear, zip ties to fasten tag to bear.
- Five-gallon bucket (2-3). Many uses – carry sand to put around bait for bear track ID, carry baits, carry water, sit on in ground blind, etc.
- Bow/gun, etc. You know your gear. No sense detailing here. However, here are a couple of things to keep in mind –
  - Archery – Set up and tune a second bow, and take it with you. There are no archery stores back in the woods, so, if you aren't already a good service technician, become as good as you can. Then take the tools and extra supplies of everything you may need to service your bow in the field.
  - Firearms – Take a second gun, just in case.
- Cases – Keep guns and bows in hard cases on ATVs and other vehicles, and have them tightly secured when traveling to your bait site. Two-tracks and swampy, muddy trails, and unexpected rocks in the path...all can knock things out of alignment. A PVC pipe will make a rugged longbow case.
  - Treestands – Each hunter should bring two or three of his own hang-on stands, plus climbing sticks. A ladder stand or two would be good.
- Safety harnesses.
- Ground blinds – **See the ground blind item in this chapter for details.**

• GATHERING INFORMATION

Contact or visit the state or province wildlife department biologist in the area you plan to hunt. Ask for good hunting areas, likely hunting pressure, success rates from recent seasons, etc. Ask them to send you bear hunting, baiting and treestand regulations for their area. Ask if they can suggest a private landowner to contact for permission to hunt on that person's land. Ask about the extent of competition in the area from other bear hunters.

Get county, regional or state/province maps to locate public land for the area you plan to hunt, and regulations on those lands. The maps should show campgrounds and hunting areas, if such designated areas exist.

• SCOUTING & STAND LOCATION
• Scout the area you will hunt, if possible...and it should be possible. Makes no sense to go into an area cold. Generally, a black bear is a lazy animal. It does not deal well with hot weather and will almost always look for damp or wet areas that give them relief from the heat. Such an area next to or in a thicket is ideal.

• Know and use the one-to-one rule if you intend to hunt from an elevated platform: for every yard from your stand to the bait, go one foot of elevation for your stand, i.e. 15 yards to stand and 15 feet up the tree.

See Chapter 5 – SCOUTING – for details.

• BAITING
• **Good baiting** and Chicago elections are similar. Chicago voting instructions are "vote early, vote often'. Good baiting is "bait early, bait often".

• If you plan to hunt over bait, ask yourself how frequently you will be able to bait before the hunt. Daily baiting produces well and keeps bait fresh. Weekend baiting has problems with stale baits.

Start baits as early as possible; a month prior to your hunt would be great. Bear will use the security of darkness to come to a bait until they feel comfortable coming in during daylight hours.

See Chapter 6 – BAITING & SCENTS – for details.

• SETTING THE BAIT
See Chapter 6 – BAITING & SCENTS – for details.

• STARTING THE HUNT
• Have the base camp set up, no matter if it is a motel room, resort cabin, tent/trailer or your own home. Having a place to call home early In the game gives stability to everything and brings order instead of chaos.

• Scent control.
  • Do not wear the clothes you will hunt in while you are cooking in camp, hauling wood or doing any camp chores.
  • Store your hunting clothes in an airtight container and get dressed to hunt in an area away from the odors of camp.
  • If shower facilities are not available, bring scent-free wipes to use prior to getting dressed to hunt. When water temperatures are warm enough, a swim is great. "Warm enough" is a sliding scale.
  • If you are driving to and from your bait on an ATV or pickup truck, get dressed after you park to walk to your bait. Carry your hunting clothes in/on the vehicle in a sealed container to be scent free and out of splashed mud and water.

• AFTER THE SHOT

- After you hit a bear you will be completely on your own.
- On a remote D-I-Y hunt, be fully prepared to get the bear out of the woods quickly and take care of the meat and hide quickly. It will be a lot of work.
- A pack frame is an important piece of equipment on a D-I-Y hunt. You may need to skin and quarter the bear to get it back to camp, and it may take more than one trip. If that is the case, cover meat left in the woods with evergreen boughs and one or two items of clothing that have plenty of your scent. Bears will move a bear they find dead to a different area and feed on it, but will be less likely to do so with a sweaty t-shirt on the carcass.
- Four people can carry out a good-sized bear on a cot or stretcher. If you tie a bear's front legs and hind legs together and hang the bear on a pole to carry it out, tie the bear's body tight to the pole. If you don't do that, the dead bear will begin swinging on the pole and sooner or later pitch everyone carrying it to the ground.
- Once back at camp, immediately begin processing the meat and hide **(See Chapter 10 for details.)**

Photo: Glenn Helgeland

• This is the result when things go right. Larry Bauman's trophy scored 20-9/16. It was sniffing a scent attractant (flavored sugar water sprayed on a small spruce) when he made the shot.

* * * * * * * * * *

GUIDED HUNTS

Using a guide service can be beneficial in many ways, but it also can create a bad experience. On a guided hunt, pre-hunt preparation is the most vital part of your hunt. A guide is only as good as the information you give him. Guides cannot read your mind, so any information you miss or forget to tell him may cause problems or even ruin the hunt.

Several years ago, my wife Sandy and I went on a Canadian hunt to video taking a bear for one of my videos. The outfitter/guide's price was good. It included meals and hunting license and a beautiful lodge. The guide would assist us in retrieving the bear and help us process the meat. He had a big walk-in cooler, freezers, everything we needed.

We learned, when shown the bait site, that it was our responsibility to get to and from the bait every day. I used a tank of gas every day going to and from the bait because it was a long distance from the lodge. This added more than $600 to the cost of our hunt.

My costly add-on easily could have been avoided had I asked enough questions prior to the hunt, particularly everything the outfitter charged for. Since that hunt I have had a checklist of questions to ask the outfitter prior to the hunt.

Another cost factor: every black bear hunter has a goal in mind, relative to bear size, for his hunt. Hunts in areas known to produce big black bears normally cost big bucks.

There are several things you can do to insure your hunt will be as pleasurable as possible. Start by assuming nothing, talking to guys who have been there and done that (and who may recommend outfitters), and preparing a list of every question you can think of. Then start looking for an outfitter who appears to have the hunting you want.

If you are booking a hunt at a consumer show, the outfitter will have pictures of the best animals taken from his area. It is that way so the outfitter can show possible clients the game trophies he has in the area he controls. But the photos probably will not show the average size of black bear you can expect. Ask the average weight of bear taken in his area. Then contact the governmental wildlife department in the area and ask the same question. This will give you an honest look at what to expect.

• *Sandy and an Ontario bear. With her, left to right, are outfitters Chris, Lorna and Terry Wood of Wood's Bowhunting. In the middle is Diesel, an Akita breed tracking dog and one of the best. The dog almost is big enough to fetch a bear as well as track it.*

Photo: Bill/Sandy Wiesner

Although it is possible to take a big bear anywhere you hunt, your odds increase when you go to an area noted for big bear. People always say there are few trophy black bear in Ontario. Nope. My wife and a lot of other people have proven opposite. For proof, check the trophy record information in Chapter 2.

Everything is all in the hands of your outfitter. The one we chose to hunt with in Ontario is strictly a bear outfitter. When you deal with someone who mainly is a fishing outfitter and bear hunts are a side job, the best information you may get is that you will catch a lot of fish.

List of unsuccessful hunts

Probably the most important question you could ask is for a list of unsuccessful hunters. I have been on bear hunts that had tough conditions, but I got my bear so I overlooked the negatives. I also have hunted at places where everything was awesome but I did not take a bear. Would I return to those places? Absolutely! If an outfitter and his crew do everything to help you have a successful hunt, you cannot ask for more. Remember, you are hunting a wild animal and things do not always go right. If you want a for-sure thing go inside a fence but that's not hunting.

Basic question: What can I expect to pay for a bear hunt?

This depends on the area and the services provided. A total-package hunt can cost from $1,500 to $3,000. If you take over once you arrive and the outfitter's work is limited to starting the baits for you, expect to pay $750 to $1,000.

Ask yourself: What can I afford? Do I want to hunt spring or fall? Which state or province do I want to hunt and, specifically, which location within that large area?

You really need to do your homework here. This cannot be overemphasized. I have seen the excitement of an upcoming hunt turn south fast because the outfitter gave incomplete or misleading information, or the hunters misinterpreted the information they received, or they had unrealistic expectations and were a bit naïve, and undoubtedly did not ask enough questions.

Pricing seems to vary from area to area. Generally, the farther west or northwest you go, the more you will pay for a hunt.

All this is not 'buyer beware', but you need to do all your homework and ask all the necessary questions. If you're not sure what's included in 'all' questions, ask a couple of people who have been there and done that.

Now begin looking for an outfitter. As you search, here are additional basic but important questions to ask:

• Nathan Ewing looks his transportation in the eye and asks it to be easy-riding and sure-footed

Photo: Bill/Sandy Wiesner

• If you use insect repellent, what brand do you use?

It makes sense to use the same repellent he uses because it is a scent the bear has become familiar with and associated with food as the guide baited.

Hunters sometimes attempt to implement different things they have read about various elements of bear hunting and want to implement some or all of those methods. However, you are paying for the services of a person who knows his hunting territory and the animals his clients hunt. You are not paying the author of a bear hunting article. I cannot count the times on guided hunts when a hunter told the outfitter "That is not the way So-and-So explained it in his article."

Let the outfitter do his job. That is what you are paying him for.

- **Can I put out scent attractants I purchased?**

No! Any time you change the scent at a bait site you are alerting the bear to a change. Bears, especially big bears, do not like change. Introducing an unfamiliar element to the bait site would be like starting the bait over.

- **I am a bowhunter; how far is the shot?** That is up to you, within reason. Sometimes an outfitter will ask you to bring your treestand so he can set it up for you at the right distance. In other cases he may have permanent stands placed and will set the bait at your effective range. In either case, tell the outfitter your effective shot distance limit. I shoot self bows, longbows and recurves most of the time, and I want to be at 15 yards or less to be effective. My sons like 20- to 25-yard shots.

• Shot distance for bowhunting usually is around 15 yards, but can be as close as 10 yards or out to 20 or 25 yards.

Photo: Glenn Helgeland

Other factors may exist. For instance, most treestands are set for right-handed archers. A left-hander in such a stand may find himself looking into spruce branches instead of the bait. A smart outfitter will have his permanent stands constructed for righties and lefties. This is easily done with two-by-fours and a board platform nailed between two trees with seats fastened to both trees.

- **Can I film the hunt?**

Seems everyone today enjoys filming the hunt. If you plan to do so, pay special attention to the bait site setup. Your ideas and the outfitter's thoughts may be different, so be sure you explain to him how you need things to be done. The bait site setup – bait location, stand location, camera location, stand(s) in place -- should be done at one time. At the least, an area should be trimmed for stand placement when the bait is started.

- **How do I get to and from my stand?**

In most cases, once the outfitter shows you to your stand it is your responsibility to get to the bait and return. What I normally do is find out if there are other stands in the area and car pool to and from the baits with the hunters on them, sharing fuel costs.

- **Is fishing available? If so, what will it cost?**

Most camps have a none-hunting fee, usually $75 to $100 per day. Boat rentals and bait are additional.

Fishing opportunities can be a huge selling point for any bear hunt. On most bear hunts, you sit the afternoons until dark. That leaves all day to look at options. Outfitters that have fishing available use it as an added perk to attempt to get your business. Ask if there is access to fishing bait and the species of fish available.

A northern Manitoba outfitter I hunted with had world class northern pike fishing. One of my friends who came along wanted only to fish and made arrangements with the outfitter. His goal was to catch a 50-inch northern pike with a fly rod. His dream came true on the fourth day. He caught and released a 51-½ inch fish, with an estimated weight of more than 30 pounds. That was a lifetime achievement he will remember forever. Another friend brought his father, whose goal was to catch artic grayling. Again, a lifetime dream was fulfilled.

- **What is needed for travel when hunting Canada?**

Now that a passport is needed to cross into Canada it has made travel to our neighbors in the north much easier. Make sure your passport is current and you have it readily available at the border. Know what you can and cannot bring into Canada. Proper paperwork must be in hand for all rifles and shotguns and NO handguns are allowed.

Arrest records are matters of concern. An arrest for drunken driving takes special paperwork to get you into Canada. Any felony leaves you home. If you have anything on an arrest record, check with the province you plan to hunt and let them know your status relative to each arrest and its resolution.

The best way to handle the crossing is to be polite and direct when answering Customs questions, and stop there. Unnecessary comments can cause delays or worse. One time my brother's wife made a smart remark to the Customs person of a nature that made them want to check our vehicle and gear. It took several hours to pack everything Customs people laid out on the blacktop during their work.

- **I am a U.S. citizen. If I get a bear in Canada and want to bring it home what can I expect?**

The CITES permit will be provided by the outfitter At the border, have your license readily available. The bear's hide and meat will need a tag; it comes with your license..

- **What is the policy when a bear is wounded?**

This varies from outfitter to outfitter. It definitely is a question to ask before you hunt, or maybe even before you book a hunt. With some outfitters, if you draw blood, that is your bear whether you recover it or not. Even if you don't recover it you're done hunting.

This makes shooting skill and self-control at the moment of truth even more important. If you are a bowhunter, devote considerable practice time to a 3-D bear target. Practice from every possible shooting position you many encounter. If you don't have a 3-D bear target, get one.

- **I would like to try a wilderness hunt on my own. Can I go through an outfitter for this?**

Yes, in fact this type of bear hunt is growing in popularity and it will save you money. It is a form of drop camp. Contact an outfitter and ask if he offers this type of hunt.

In this arrangement, the outfitter starts several baits prior to your arrival.

• *Sometimes an outfitter will set you up in a drop camp. This lovely northern Minnesota camp included a boat and canoe, which proved handy for bringing a tagged bear to camp..*

Photo: Glenn Helgeland

You take over when you get there. Having a bait started saves valuable time and gives you the best opportunity to take a bear. You supply the tent or camper, food and all the necessities. He will put you in a pre-determined spot and supply the bait. I have tried to haul my own bait, but it is not a good idea. I may not use the same type of bait the outfitter is using. Such a change is like starting the bait all over, and it is difficult, at best, to haul the bait any distance.

If you go this route, be sure you have the necessary materials for the hunt and for meat and hide care. This hunt takes more pre-hunt preparation than a fully guided hunt.

• Can I bring a gun and a bow on a guided hunt?

In most cases, yes, but check with the outfitter. Some states or provinces may not allow a firearm on a bowhunter's person while hunting. When set up for a bow shot, a gun shot at that distance will really be close range.

I can remember only one time I needed a gun on a bow setup. I was filming a friend's spring bowhunt. We watched a nice bear walk the perimeter of the bait two nights in a row without a shot. I did not realize it was a boar looking for a receptive female and not interested in feeding. However, had a female come to the bait he probably would have followed her into bow range.

On the third evening of the hunt the bear showed again, circling the perimeter of the bait. My friend took it with a rifle.

Of a practical nature, the problem with having both hunting arms is that at the moment of truth you may become indecisive and spoil your chance with too much movement hanging up one item and picking up another. Far better to keep it as uncomplicated as possible and stay with one hunting arm unless the decision to use bow or gun is a no-brainer.

• Which rifle or shotgun action is the best for bear hunting?

This is not that important an issue. The most important point is to use the one you are most familiar with. Your deer hunting rifle should work perfectly if is the right caliber and you're shooting a good bullet weight. When the moment of truth presents itself, the firearm you are familiar with allows you to focus solely on the bear. If your current rifle is not right for taking a large tough, heavy-pelted, big-boned animal, be sure the gun you choose has the same action as your current rifle. A heavy shotgun slug and lower power scope work well, too, of course.

Bears move silently through the woods. You may look up and there it stands, looking up at you trying to figure out what you are, or already on the bait in shooting position. When that happens, it is easy to be confused by an unfamiliar firearm.

• **I would like to hunt bear different ways. Is this possible on one guided hunt?**

Because baits are normally sat from late afternoon until dark, you have all day to try spot-and-stalk or calling. This can be an enjoyable way to maximize your actual hunting time and quite possibly learn more about bears and bear hunting.

Ask your outfitter before the hunt whether these options are permissible. It is entirely his decision. I have found they are likely to help you if they know in advance. Bring the proper equipment, from clothing to footwear, that will allow you to try different hunting methods most effectively.

• **Do you suggest a spring or fall hunt?**

Spring will allow you to experience bears in different behavior and activity modes (breeding season activity, feeding frenzies), and the possibility of seeing more bears. Also, pelts are prime right out of hibernation up to the days weather turns warm and bears begin rubbing to get rid of their winter coat.

Spring timing is very important. The change of seasons dictates when bears will move the best. Be aware that breeding season timing can differ a bit from year to year. All the more reason to remain in close contact with your outfitter. Although spring hunts can have an unpredictable atmosphere, the upside is that you can benefit from that unpredictability.

Hunting in the fall has its advantages. Baits can be very active because bears are feeding heavily, adding fat for their hibernation. They will be up to 25 percent heavier now than in the spring. Their coats are normally in prime shape

• **What physical condition must I be in?**

As good as is necessary. Period.

Recently, I traveled to Wyoming in search of an elusive color phase bear. I walked for several months before going on the hunt. There are no hills to speak of where I live in Wisconsin.

In the West, everything seems to be straight up and straight down. Add the elevation of 11,000 feet and you are talking a whole new issue that I had

• *Crossing this bridge was an adventure. So was walking up the mountain.*

Photo: Bill/Sandy Wiesner

not properly prepared for. To set up baits in this country, you have to put more effort into the hunt than I anticipated.

I was told to walk as much as possible prior to the early June Wyoming hunt. I did! In camp, it was hard to sleep the night before a hunt with so much promise for the fulfillment of a long-sought goal of tagging a color phase bear other than black. All my mind could see were the trail camera photos the outfitter had sent me of colored bear.

The next morning's plan was to drop off my two friends with their horses and guide to climb to their stands on horseback. I was told we would hike into my stand. I asked why? The outfitter simply told me he had no Clydesdales in his stables. He smiled a bit when he said it, but not a lot. When I arrived at my stand the first night, I asked to be left there until the next day's hunt, just bring a couple sandwiches please. I hunted that stand three nights; no bear.

The fourth night I was told we were going to hunt a stand much easier to approach. Yessss! However (a term that always means trouble), the outfitter forgot to mention one small item -- a turbulent mountain stream to cross. They decided to reinforce the two trees already in place that they called a bridge with a couple more trees, just for me.

I shakily got across the makeshift bridge with the help of the outfitter and finally arrived at my destination. All afternoon all I could think about was going back over that bridge in the dark. Bears were just barely on my mind.

It was a great hunt. I did not get my bear; others in our group did.

A friend told me about a hunt he labeled 'The Bear Hunt From Hell'. It was a late May Western hunt, more river float than hunt. The few bears out were still on top of the mountains feeding on grass instead of down on the slopes within view and within range from the river. Hunters were urged to climb to the top, which no one had been led to expect, and to shoot if they saw a bear, even if it was 400 yards or more away. A couple of guys tried it. They saw a bear, out nearly 500 yards, but resisted instructions to shoot. When they came back down, mutterings of "...never again..." were heard. Those two bears were the only bears seen by anyone all week. The guys figured out later that, had they shot, the outfitter could have claimed "X% of clients had shooting". That's not the same as high percentage shots and a lot different from "X% of clients filled their tag". They also were not allowed to use .270 rifles because too many clients using that caliber had wounded bears and not recovered them. That's not necessarily the rifle's fault; ballistics are basically the same as a .30-06. At those distances a bear is a little black blob with no distinct aiming spots, and that could be only one factor.

* * * * * * * * *

BARKING UP A BEAR

Chasing bear with dogs sparks the most controversy in the bear hunting world. You either like it or you don't. For those who don't like it, the attitude usually is "It's ok, but it's not for me."

Hound hunters are dedicated to their dogs; many treat their dogs like family. Their dogs require hard and constant work to feed, keep healthy and rain. In this process, a strong bond develops between hunter and dogs. Some hunters freely admit they hunt bears so they can work their dogs.

Where to begin?

With the dogs, naturally. A hound man has to have the right type of dog, one that will pass all the stringent tests required to become a good bear dog. If you want an opinion on which breed of dog makes the best bear hound, don't ask a hound man. Talking hound breeds with hound men is worse than talking religion. It can become a touchy subject. Bluetpicks, Redticks, Walkers, curs, Plotts and plain old mixed breeds can produce excellent bear dogs. There are good and bad in every breed, and that's to be expected.

Training a bear dog is hard work involving hours of the hunter's time, spread over days and months. Normally, a young dog is run with experienced dogs in hopes the youngster catches on to how the game is played. If a dog is too aggressive, his stay as a bear dog can be short lived. Once the youngster has proven his keep, a new member is added to the pack.

What makes the best dog, male or female? For the answer, read the previous paragraph and replace "which breed?" with "male or female".

Watching good bear dogs work, whether male or female, is an absolute pleasure.

Characteristics in dogs can range from being cold nosed, which means they can pick up on older tracks, to a good tree dog, which is a dog that will push the bear until it trees and stay there holding the bear until the hunters arrive. If a dog has all these attributes, he or she is a keeper.

The owner of these hardy animals knows exactly what each one of his dogs can accomplish. To watch them use each hound as the hunt unfolds is something every bear enthusiast should witness.

The action of the chase is what dog hunting is all about to these houndmen. They are there to witness how each of their dogs performs, from the start of the chase to the finish of the hunt.

Photo: Bill Wiesner

• *A 'treed' bark has a different tone from a chase baying. It's a thrill to hear.*

Records show that fewer bear are taken by dog hunters than by bait sitters. All bear hunters should be aware of this fact.

Typical Season for the Hound Hunter

Baits are placed early in the year to assess bear quantity and quality in the area to be hunted and to better keep track of bear movement. Hunters normally sand baits so they know the size of bear or bears hitting each bait.

If a big bear is hitting, hunters normally do not run that bear, hoping it w be there when season opens.

Training season starts in summer when air temperatures are high. Runn bear will take place in the mornings while dew is still on the grass and air is cooler. Baits are checked before daylight. When a hot track is fou dogs are released at first light, hoping to jump the bear. Once the chas on, they run the bear until it trees or the dogs catch it on the ground. T training period conditions hounds for the fall hunt and gives houndsmen idea what is in the area.

Bears can tree in 50 yards or run all day. Younger bears and slimmer be seem to be the ones that can go forever. Larger and older bear will tree turn and fight the dogs; treeing is difficult for larger bears because they just plain too big. Bears fattened up for the winter won't run far beca they're too fat and get overheated and tired.

- **One medium-sized bear treed. Pull the dogs off? Probably.**

I have seen bear that were jumped at first light, not tree by dark, and had to catch the dogs. From my experience, only about half the bears cha go up a tree. Of those treed during hunting season, only about one in th is taken.

Three in the morning is a popular time to the hound hunter. Baits checked and if there are no desirable bear to run we go roading -- driv dirt roads and, with flashlights, looking for fresh tracks crossing the road

A strike dog, normally the one with the best nose, is placed on carpeted hood of the truck. If the track found is fresh the dog will sound The track is checked and a decision made to run it or not.

Hunting bears with dogs goes from the low of lows to wide open minutes. Complete silence on the radio can change to talking non-s and even shouting. Driving at a snail's pace can quickly turn into a Du of Hazzard run as everyone races to assemble and position themselve watch for the bear. Radios are going non-stop. This is the excitemer hound hunting for black bear.

When a bear is treed during the training season, pictures are taken the dogs are leashed. Depending on the time of day, another bear ma may not be run. Hunts start out being short and will increase in length as hounds get into better shape. The concern is always directed to the dogs care is always taken to insure its health and safety.

Another safety concern: where there are wolves, there will be wolf attacks on dogs. Attacks usually target dogs that fall behind the rest of the pack during the chase, such as older dogs that tire easily, and young dogs that are distracted by other scent and separate from the pack.

Bear hunting with hounds is the total package.

Do's, Don'ts, Plans and Gear

If you plan to hunt with a hound hunter, always be sure you understand the instructions they give you as the hunter. Your hunt will run smoothly if you pay attention.

Choosing an outfitter for hound hunting needs special attention. I strongly suggest you contact hunters who have used a guide's services. You are completely at the guide's mercy; doing your homework prior to the hunt is paramount. Hound hunters can be a different breed of individuals and they accept that, so be ready to encounter people who may come off differently from other hunters. This is not a bad thing, you are just dealing with people totally committed to their sport. That dedication results in your enjoyment of the hunt.

Never be afraid to tell your outfitter what you can or cannot do. If you are not good at firing at a walking or running bear, let him know. They are good at what they do but are not mind readers. The better the communication you have with your guide, the better results you will experience.

Safety has to be top priority at all times. The fast-paced action is so different from any other type of hunting that you can easily become preoccupied with the action and forget about safety

Your physical condition is a factor in bear hunting, but it applies heaviest, no pun intended, to hound hunting. You must be able to be in the right place at the right time when bear hunting with dogs. No guide can help you with your ability to get from Point A to Point B. His effort may fall short because of your inability to finish. Your success is a direct result of your pre-hunt preparation.

Type of footwear is important. Your ability to move around is paramount. Wear lightweight waterproof boots, because you probably will spend time in water. Include boot dryers in your what-to-bring list.

Bring several changes of clothing. You will sweat while following dogs through standard bear escape terrain. Dress in layers. Cool mornings can turn to hot days on a spring or fall hunt, and following dogs can get much warmer than riding in a truck. A good rain suit should be in your pack, just in case. Insect repellent may come in handy. Seems the best bear hunting is always when the bugs are at their best.

The type of bow or gun is personal choice, with a couple of guiding factors. Big bears do not like to tree because it is difficult or impossible for them. They bay at the base of a tree or in front of a big rock, or whatever object will keep dogs from getting at them from behind. With an excited, active pack of hounds and a defensive bear trying to face all of them and able to break and run at any moment, and you possibly out of breath from trying to get to the bayed bear quickly before it breaks and runs, you have to make a quick shoot-or-no-shoot decision in what may be thick brush at

• *Bryan and a Wisconsin gun kill. He uses a .45/70 that's quick handling, should a bayed bear break and run.*

a moving target. A short-barreled, quickly aimed gun fits this situation very well. My son Bryan carries a .45/70 on dog hunts for such instances.

The general rule of thumb is, of course, be familiar with your equipment. On a hound hunt, you have enough things to think about in the progress of the hunt without worrying about unfamiliar equipment at the moment of truth.

* * * * * * * * * *

SPOT-AND-STALK BEAR

There sometimes is confusion over the terms 'stalking' and 'still hunting'. For the sake of clarity, 'still hunting' is a means of slowly and silently cruising the woods looking for game, and 'stalking' is what you do once the game is spotted and you are attempting to get within shooting range.

WHICH METHOD OF BEAR HUNTING IS THE MOST DIFFICULT?

Stalking and spot-and-stalk hunting, hands down. You are going to the bear, unlike attempting to bring the bear to you. If done right, at the end of a day of spot-and-stalk, you will be exhausted, mentally and physically, from self-imposed, all-day tension, if for no other reason. It isn't our nature to move extremely slowly for extended periods of time, while at the same time having all our senses on full alert. We are depending on our skills of movement control and full focus on the goal far more than in any other style of the hunt. The difficulty of spot-and-stalk bear hunting makes it a true challenge and certainly adds dimension to bear hunting. Our family's success rate is about 15 percent.

Patience is a virtue in all hunting, but especially so in spot-and-stalk hunting. Always begin a stalk in a deliberate, controlled manner, and keep it that way. Be sure, with every move you make, you are aware of what the bear is doing. Then react to its movement or non-movement. If there's no movement, try to figure out why. Wait. Let the bear take the lead. That will tell you what you need to do to get in position for a shot.

This style of bear hunting is not as common in the Upper Midwest or East as it is in the West, although some areas in eastern-most Canadian provinces are relatively open or wide open tundra and thus can offer spot-and-stalk opportunities. In Wisconsin, Minnesota and Michigan, and in Ontario and Quebec, bears are always in the presence of many food sources. Acorns, berries and sometimes corn, to name a few, are available in a number of areas, making your chances of locating bears more difficult. If you don't know where bears are feeding, it's pretty much game over.

Best settings for spot-and-stalk are along rivers, power line grassy strips or open grassy slopes in the spring when grass is green, edges of woods that skirt a crop field, and directly in a cornfield.

In the West, there are not nearly as many food sources available, the terrain is more open and lends itself to spot-and-stalk hunting. Bear often need to roam great distances to find food. The area can be surveyed from greater distances; you can plan your final approach from a greater distance and with less chance of being detected. Try to move in cover, because bears almost always will graze on grass relatively close to the security of cover. If this isn't feasible, have a scoped rifle, binoculars and a rangefinder in hand.

Bears generally move best in early morning and late afternoon, looking to feed. The exception to that is the spring breeding season, when males are in constant movement.

Maximum shot distances to expect: Rifle - 250 to 300 yards; muzzleloader (in-line) – 150 yards; muzzleloader (old style) - 75 yards; crossbow - 50 yards; compound bow - 40 yards; recurve bow and longbow - 30 yards.

• RANGEFINDER

A good rangefinder will back you up, eliminating the guesswork that could lead to a poor hit or a missed shot. Unlike sitting at a bait where you know your shot distance, or shooting a bear treed by dogs, a stalk hunt has unknown distances, differences in terrain types, variations in elevation, and the surprise factor in short-range situations in cover. That all adds up to a great challenge.

• BINOCULARS

Binoculars give you a couple of benefits on a stalk-and-spot hunt. You can more accurately see at a greater distance exactly what the bear is doing, check out your approach path beyond right in front of you and note options, identify the sex of bear at a longer distance, and make your move when it is to your advantage.

You want to bring the binoculars into action quickly and with little motion. A binocular harness that holds your binoculars in place on your chest is one option. A large pocket on your shirt or jacket, positioned so it won't interfere with your bowstring, is another option.

Compact binoculars are not so bulky and weigh less, of course. A

• You can hold binoculars steadier and longer this way. Cradle the binoculars on your palms, hook your index fingers over your eyebrow ridges, push your thumbs against your cheekbones, and push your arms against your chest. Move the focusing wheel with your second fingers as needed. This is particularly helpful for glasses wearers, because you won't need to push the rubber eyecups against the lenses. This is a benefit any time and a huge benefit when you're hunting anywhere wind blows dust; you no longer will get scratch rings on your lenses

compact 8x42 or 10x32 is a good way to go. The eight-power will be fin for bowhunters, due to shorter-range operations. Rifle hunters looking an shooting at longer distances may want the higher magnification.

For maximum steadiness, rest your thumbs on your cheekbones, th barrels of the binocular loosely against the outside base of your hand, an your curved index fingers on your eyebrow ridges. Tuck your elbows again your chest. This is rock solid.

Optics will help you avoid excessive contact with the area the bear may be ir

In addition to binoculars, I like to use spotting scopes when I'm drivin and looking for bears in the early spring. Sometimes I find actual sign longer distances. In the fall, I try to stay in my truck and skirt a crop fiel I plan to hunt. I look for tracks, scat and the location of bear entrances t the field then plan according for what will some intense short-range spot and-stalk.

• CLOTHING

In spot and stalk, the goal is to be non-distinguishable from you surroundings, by image and by odor. You do that by breaking your outline positioning yourself next to a tree trunk or bushes and by making yourse and your clothing as scent-free as possible.

• Camouflage everything. Wear camouflage or plaid colors that matc the background of the terrain you are hunting. You don't have to spend fortune on camouflage and scent-free clothing. More times than not, I mi camouflage clothing with black and green plaid clothing.

• Face paint or camouflage head-net and gloves are necessary. You extremities move more than any other part of your body. Keep in mind that head-net may obstruct your vision and anchor point at the moment of trutl

• For maximum scent control, wear carbon-impregnated base layer an outer layer clothing. A more economical way to go is to get powdere carbon, available in several brands, mix with water and dip your existin hunting clothing in that treatment.

Hunting Style

• Carry a daypack with a bottle of water, a first aid kit, a sandwich and snack, and hygiene necessities so you can spend the day hunting. You need to be prepared to face all adversities in the field. This means insect repellent, sunglasses (but be careful of reflection catching a bear's attention), knife (if not on your belt) and rope. Put a camera in your pack, too. You'll want photos of your trophy right where it falls.

• COMPASS / GPS

We're talking spot-and-stalk hunting, meaning there may be sneaking around the woods not paying attention to directions.

Use a compass. Or GPs and mark your base. Whatever helps you know where you are and helps get you back to camp when you want to get back to camp on a route you want to take.

• FOOTWEAR

When you are sneaking on a bear, your total focus must be on your intended target, but at the same time you need to know where you're stepping. If you are trying to watch your step and focus on the bear simultaneously, your attention isn't really focused anywhere. This, unfortunately, can cause you to snap a twig and spook the bear.

For best results, and to give yourself more confidence, wear boots that let you feel what you are stepping on. I have custom-made boots with a soft elk hide sole. When I put my foot down, I step on the outside edge of my foot first and roll the rest of my foot softly to the ground. This minimal movement allows me to feel an obstruction and step elsewhere, if need be, before putting full weight on my foot. I avoid snapping a twig or making any other noticeable sound.

Boot soles should be smooth or pebble-grain or have shallow grooves. Deep lugs in the soles are no good; they catch everything, make noise, and can make you trip.

• PRACTICE MORE PARTS OF THE HUNT THAN JUST SHOOTING

Once you have equipment and clothing ready, try to get to the woods for practice. Practice with all the equipment you plan to use, dress in your hunting cloths, shoot broadheads, kneel down and shoot, practice standing slowly and lifting your arms slowly to take the shot, practice using binoculars and range finders with minimal movement. If you will be wearing a head-net when hunting, practice with it so you have a true picture of the sight picture through the net. This effort will allow you to make the needed changes, put your stalk together and be most efficient at the moment of truth. Practice will give you confidence in your gear and yourself, allowing you to focus on the stalk and the shot. The more ready you are, the better your chance of success.

It is important to know you will have shooting opportunities at various distances.

With a bow, expect shots to be 40 yard or less. If anything near 40 yards is out of your effective range because of your equipment selection or your own shooting skills limitations, you will need to move closer. Or at least try to do so. At 40 yards a bear's eyesight is not good when looking at stationary objects, but all its other senses are still in good working order.

With a rifle, your shot may be 200 yards or more but more often will be closer to 100 yards. Practice at those distances and be sure you practice at a BLACK target resembling a bear. Of course, this is after you use a bulls-eye target to sight in the gun. At those distances a specific aiming spot is tough to pick out, but that's what you must do. If you shoot in the middle of the black spot, hoping for the best, you most likely will only wound the bear.

Timing is hugely important in spot-and-stalk. Spot-and-stalk is a series of slow, deliberate movements and a lot of waiting patiently, tense and alert. Never rush movements, but be able to move, and move the right way, the instant an opportunity arises. Call it a quick response to move slowly. Move only when the bear is feeding or its attention is on other bear or birds or other animals in the area, and move very slowly when you do move. One of the biggest mistakes is trying to move too much at one time; it may take you 15 to 20 minutes to move 15 yards. All motions must be slow, because they're more difficult to detect. Most bears bust the hunter near the end of the stalk, simply because the hunter becomes impatient, or gets sore muscles, or reaches a point of boredom.

No matter where you spot and stalk a bear, always use any cover provided and try to stay in the shadows. Bear do not see stationary objects well, but they can detect movement relatively easily. Work the wind, stay hidden and always be deliberate in your approach to prey.

I was not successful on a spot-and-stalk hunt until after about a dozen failed attempts. Every time I went out I learned by my mistakes, such as moving too fast and spooking the bear at the last minute, or not being ready to shoot because my arrow was still in the quiver, or not paying close enough attention to the wind, or focusing only on the intended bear when there were multiple bears feeding or moving nearby. My arrow should have been nocked; I should have been mindful of wind direction at all times because it can swirl and end the stalk instantly; and when there are multiple bears in the area the ignored bear is the one that busts you in mid-stalk.

It was a spring hunt in Ontario when the province still allowed spring bear hunts. I arrived in camp early, but the baits were not being touched. I had all the necessary spot-and-stalk equipment to sneak within range of a bear just out of hibernation.

Canada calls their power lines hydro lines. I traveled back roads glassing hydro lines for bear feeding on grass. This is a perfect time to ambush a bear. Bears feed on grass for only a short period each spring right after they come out of hibernation. If you are geared up and recognize this opportunity, your chances for spot-and-stalk success can probably be at its best.

I finally saw an average male feeding on grass on the hydro line. After glassing from a distance his movement and the cover and terrain between him and me, I mentally marked his location and made my stalk plan. This meant circling downwind through the woods, keeping far enough into the woods to be well hidden and avoid alarming him but to stay on track toward his position, using my binoculars all the way. As I neared the edge of the hydro-line, I stepped even more carefully and softly, continually glassing to pin down its exact position. When the top of its back came into view as i fed on the grass, I began my final approach even more carefully. It took a while – one or two years, it seemed -- to close the last 50 yards that would put me in shooting position. At 25 yards, the bear put its head down to feed. I drew and sent the arrow on its way to the aiming spot. My arrow hit that spot and the bear went down within sight.

SPRING HUNTS

In the spring, right after leaving their dens, bears feed on grasses to get rid of the over-winter plug in their intestines and get their digestive system into gear again. Their system is not yet ready for more substantial fare. Therefore, look for bear to be feeding in power line openings, which normally have nice green grasses early in the spring.

• In the spring, the edges of grassy slopes and power line openings are great places to watch for feeding bears.

Photo: Glenn Helgeland

Long-range scouting of these power line openings will tell you where to hunt. This means mileage and optics. Good optics (binoculars and spotting scope) are necessary to locate the bear, then determine if it is one you care to pursue. Try to determine where the bear is entering the power line opening so you can be set up on the downwind side of that point when it comes into view.

Keep a close eye on the bear's travel routes and movement from day to day. It is best to glass the bear more than one time to determine its entry timing and movement pattern. A bear can move out of an area in a day's time, due to lack of food, unwanted interaction with other animals, or too much human and vehicle presence, or maybe just because. There can be any number of reasons. It will, however, return to the same area for several consecutive days, maybe not to the same spot but to the same area.

A great thing about a spring spot-and-stalk hunt is the simple fact that, if you arrive early for a hunt but the bears are not yet hitting baits, it is obvious they are eating grass. This gives you the opportunity to hunt bear in a different manner while you await the more traditional bears on baits activity to begin. This doubling-up of hunting styles was the case with me for years in Canada at my friend's outfitting territory.

Another perspective: in the West you can expect the most success with spot-and-stalk, because there is more open and semi-open terrain. This means that in many instances you don't need to go through all the work of scouting and setting up baits and stands. In fact, baiting is illegal in some western states.

Once you are comfortable with the result of a day or more of surveillance scouting on a particular shooter bear, plan the stalk. This may be as simple as setting up on a spot you feel a bear will frequent and waiting until a bear shows, or actually moving in on a bear you have spotted.

After discovering a bear's tendencies and movement pattern, I have gone to a specific-yet-general area and waited for a bear to come into view. Once it did, I began spot-and-stalk. This doesn't mean the bear came into range; it simply means that I had put myself in a location that increased my chance for a spot-and-stalk opportunity. I guess you could say I met the bear halfway, but it didn't know it.

If you have a bear patterned, moved in before daylight and set up to wait for it, but the bear comes in downwind, retreat as quietly and quickly as possible to get out of the air current moving from you to the bear, hope the bear does not bust you as you move out, and hope for a better day.

Suppose the bear comes out down the line from where you anticipated it would enter the area, but the wind is in your favor. You are still in the game. Now you have to decide whether to let the bear feed to you, or whether you have the opportunity (and necessity) to begin a stalk. If you're motionless, not moving, there's less chance you will be busted. If a stalk appears to be the best decision, carefully survey the area between you and the place where you want to intercept the bear within good shot range. Let the cover and terrain make your decision. Do not force anything; take what is in front of you and use it accordingly. Of course, this is important in any stalking situation.

I have stalked bears where I needed to go only 100 yards for the shot, but it took several hours to get there. If you cannot move, you may have to wait until the bear moves in order to close the distance.

Study the bear's movements to understand when it is possible to move. Look for the bear's head movement. Watch it as it feeds, because then it will not be on full alert. You will see it in every imaginable position as it moves around. Note how long it usually keeps its head down. This can be your key to the most opportune time to move. Never move on a bear while it is moving. If the bear suddenly changes direction and starts to move in your direction, wait it out.

FALL HUNTS

Areas bears frequent in the fall are much smaller than those frequented in the spring; activity is concentrated. Spring brings large areas of grasses versus berry patches in the fall. Fall offers a wide variety of mast crops that bears feed on heavily to put on winter fat

Concentrate in the fall on crops that can be called 'bear ready'. This doesn't necessary mean ripe grains or fruit, but usually it does.

Berries normally are the first crop that draws bears in the fall. Raspberries, blackberries, blueberries and thimbleberries are relatively common in the north. They all ripen at different times in early fall; monitor them closely for bear activity. Blueberry patches are normally much larger than other types of berries. This gives the bear a larger area to enter and exit the berry patch

There is, however, a timing downside to berry patches. Berries are ar early season crop and may already have been swept clean before hunting season opens. This makes berry patch monitoring even more of a necessity.

When you find a berry patch that has been hit by bears, look for two things: 1) where the bear entered and exited the berries and 2) whether there are berries remaining. Tracks will indicate where the bear enters and exits the berries, and remaining berries guarantee the bears' return.

Scat is another sign. Bears normally defecate as they leave the berry patch or shortly after leaving.

Problem with berry patches is that not all situations offer a decent stalking opportunity. If you're waiting at Site A the bear may enter at Site B. So you switch position and the next night the bear enters at Site A.

If conditions are not right for a stalk, set up an ambush on an entry trail. You may get a close shot at a bear coming in on the runway, or you may have a stalk opportunity if it enters the berry patch at another point. Play the game but give yourself options; it's all hunting.

Cornfields

Corn is a good example. Bear devour corn and flatten a lot of it before it is ready for harvest, creating considerable economic loss to the farmer growing that corn. Bears practically live in the corn while feasting on it. In my home state of Wisconsin, corn crop damage caused by bears is enormous. As a result, farmers often invite bear hunters with open arms.

• Cornfields in the fall are ideal spot-and-stalk venues. Go cross-row, slowly, and peek ahead to assess each row.

Photo: Glenn Helgeland

I once asked a farmer permission to hunt one of his cornfields. He quickly said yes, then added, "A bear is doing one of two things -- he has destroyed something and is leaving, or he is on his way to destroying something!"

When a bear finds a cornfield ready for eating, it will eat as much as its stomach will allow, then often roll in the crop, apparently for sheer pleasure, knocking it down and destroying more than it ate. I haven't heard any logical explanation of this and have no idea why they do it. It may be a way to let other bears know that the crop belongs to it by leaving its scent and very visible evidence, too.

The farther north you travel the more mast crops you find, such as acorns, other nuts and berries, and fewer farm crops.

Hunting standing corn is a different matter, because a cornfield probably is the best place to stalk a bear. Timing is critical. Corn is ready for bears before it is ready to harvest.

Long-range scouting will build a good foundation for close-up scouting and add to your success. Get in position back from the corner of a field close to where you feel the bear will show and so you can watch an end and side of the field without disturbing anything. This can be from a knoll or other small rise in the ground or in tall weeds, anywhere you can get a birds-eye view of the area. Get in position before daylight and try to pinpoint where bears enter and leave the corn. Keep in mind that the bear may not come out at the same spot every time, so keep your distance to get a good view of a broader area.

In initial checking, tracks also will help you identify movement patterns but will not give you a time frame.

If the corn is in an area you can't watch from a distance, look for sign and set up trail cameras to be your eyes. Look for tracks, scat and corn that has been knocked down (usually in large areas). Raccoons also knock down corn, but not big areas as bear do.

Once you have identified bear sign, implement a plan. Wind is the dominant consideration, of course. Corn is noisy. The more noise it is making because of wind, the better your odds of remaining undetected.

Enter the corn near where bears are entering. Most bears enter at the ends of fields, not the sides. Enter at a 90-degree angle to their entry path. You want to stay behind the bear, so do not go far down the side of the corn before beginning your cross-row stalk. Peek into each row before you move your body into that row. Look in both directions. If you see no bear, step into the row.

Continue to stalk each row until you spot a bear or come out the other side of the field. If you are crossing the wind, move down the cornfield to the point where you could see while in the corn. If you are walking into the wind you need to walk around the field in order to enter with the wind in your face.

When you spot a bear, the real hunt begins. Once again, move slowly and deliberately. Survey the situation, think it through and plan your final approach. (This applies more to a bow hunt than to a gun hunt. If you're hunting with a gun in a cornfield, at this point the hunt is pretty much over.) Make sure you identify possible hang-ups and obstructions in the surrounding area so you can get in range as quietly as possible. Pull your head back to the row you're standing in, shoulder your gun or draw your bow, then (with firearm) silently lean or step (with a bow) into the same row as the bear, aim and shoot.

I once took a cornfield bear shortly after daylight. All conditions were in my favor, and we knew a good bear was in the corn, habitually feeding early in the morning. I shot the bear with my bow at less than 15 yards while it was occupied with the tender corn. Its skull measured 21-4/16; it weighed more than 400 pounds.

Dog hunters frequently check standing corn looking for tracks and an opportunity to jump a corn-loving black bear.

Acorns

Once acorns fall, bait hunters find that bears hit baits much less often or not at all. How best to counter this? Find a concentration of acorn-producing oak trees and set a stand there, or try to spot-and-stalk bear in the area of the greatest mast crop concentration. You might try to find dog hunters to jump a bear from the acorn feeding area, but it's difficult making last minute arrangements.

It seems that as a bear gets older and bigger, it feeds where the food is easy to get to, requires little movement while feeding and is most plentiful. Kind of reminds me of myself!

Oats

Black bears hammer oats fields in the northern areas of farm country in Canada, up beyond corn growing country. They hit oats when the grain heads are in the 'milk' stage of development. Squeeze an oat grain at that time and you will squeeze out a thick, white fluid that does, indeed, look like milk. Oat grains at this stage of development are nutritious and palatable to bears. Ripe grain heads are not. Eating oats in the milk stage must make bears extremely happy, for they often roll around in the oats where they have just fed, flatting big areas of oats, absolutely ruining the grain, causing considerable economic damage. That factor, understandably, aggravates farmers in those areas.

One other great thing about bear hunting in or around agricultural crop fields: the farmer most likely will be more than happy to get on his tractor, hook up a wagon and fetch your bear for you.

* * * * * * * * * *

HUNTING FROM GROUND BLINDS

Hunting from ground blinds opens a new chapter in how exciting bear hunting can be. The chance to look a bear in the eyes and hear it breathing close to your blind puts a new perspective on the bear/hunter relationship.

There is a natural fear of bears, and being right on the playing field with them can be overwhelming at first. However, remain calm and take a deep breath; there is nothing to fear. That bear is there to feed on the bait you are watching. Because of a bear's inquisitive nature, it may wander near the blind to check you out. This happens, and in my experiences the result always is the same – it goes back to feeding without incident.

Ground blinds allow you to get away with more movement, which is a big plus. However, your ability to see is more restricted than from a tree stand. Ground blinds are warmer, too, trapping your body heat and blocking the wind.

A ground blind for bear does not have to be buried in brush, as you often do for deer. Turkeys and bears are the only two big game species I know of not bothered by a blind set up in the open. However, I still like to put the blind among brush or branches to break the outline a bit.

Find and note approach routes to the bait, then put your blind in an area that avoids travel corridors and approach routes. Set up the blind so you can shoot to the bait without needing to clear much brush, if any. You do not want to change the area after bears are already feeding on the bait.

No matter what you do, there may be surprises.

I was hunting one time in northern Saskatchewan, in the middle of a spruce grove. The grove was fairly open. My wife and I were well into a long wait. I was asleep in my chair when Sandy tapped me on the leg.

"I heard some breathing right back of the blind," she whispered.

I quietly opened the closed window and let out a startled yell that probably could have been heard in Manitoba. The bear was INCHES from the open window. That is the truth, not an exaggeration.

The last we saw of that bear, it was headed west as fast as it could run.

Since then, I have had several encounters with bear near the blind, watched them inspect everything, including the blind, and then walk to the bait or leave without incident.

Always respect a bear, but you do not have to fear it.

HUNTING BLIND

• Be sure you can move around inside the blind from window to window without interference.

• The blind material must be quiet; plastic-style blind skins do not work.

• The blind should be easy, fast and quiet to set up.

• Once the blind is up, the material should be tight and not be able to move in the wind. Loose material will spook a bear.

• You do not want the bear to see your outline in the blind, nor see you move. No matter which blind you use, be certain the interior is totally black. Always were dark camouflage clothing; black clothing from the waist up also works.

• **Windows**

Blinds normally have a number of windows of different sizes and heights, some horizontal, some vertical. Vertical windows allow shooting at different distances.

All windows must open and close easily and quietly. Velcro tabs are not a good window fastener choice; they are too noisy. Look for a blind with hook-style window fasteners, so you can open and close windows with no noise. Also, with the hook window fastener, you can twist window material in the middle to have the window partially open. You need only a narrow slit at the right height to be able to better observe the surroundings.

NEVER sit so you are in line with two open windows. You will be silhouetted. An approaching bear could catch any move you make. This usually is best handled by having all back windows shut and side windows open only in the front part (for checking approach trails) or not at all.

Size

If you gun hunt, a compact blind will be fine because the only movement you make will be to lift and aim the gun. You already will have it resting on a shooting stick at the proper level, so you may not even need to lift it. Sit far enough back, away from any open windows, that neither you nor the gun barrel can be seen. Do not have the gun barrel sticking out the window. On the other hand, you will want the muzzle at least even with the window, or

Photo: Sandy Wiesner

Photo: Sandy Wiesner

• *Use a large enough blind and set it back in brush or shadows if possible. Bears don't pay particular attention to a blind set in the open, but they are a curious animal so why tempt them.*

• *Test inside clearance for bow and/ or gun. You don't want a bow's limb tip slamming against a blind wall.*

Photo: Bill Wiesner

Photo: Sandy Wiesner

• *Here's why I take the blind with me every night when I leave the bait and re-set it the next day. Bears wrecked a couple of blinds when I left them in place. Replacing blinds is expensive.*

• *Vertical windows give a clear sight picture of the bait and allow for any aiming adjustment needed. Any of your movement will be better covered than with a horizontal window.*

slightly outside it, when you squeeze the trigger. Failure to do that could lead to an ear-damaging, extremely loud tent upon the shot. (It could be worse. You could be sitting in a dry metal stock tank in prairie country looking at a pronghorn and forgetting to get scope AND muzzle above the tank rim before squeezing the trigger. This has been done. The guy who did it said he couldn't hear for two days.)

If you are a bow hunter, there are two types of blinds to consider. With a compound, a smaller blind will fill the bill; just be sure it is tall enough for top limb tip clearance and you are sitting high enough for bottom limb tip clearance.

With recurves and longbows, height of the blind's top and width must be considered. Most recurve and longbow shooters cant their bow. This brings blind width into consideration for limb tip clearance on sides and top. The longer limbs of these two bow styles may require a taller blind than you would use with a firearm or a compound bow.

You MUST test every possible bow movement, including drawing, to determine exactly where you will sit for complete clearance in every direction when you draw. Do not get set up too far back from the open window(s). If you're in a corner of the blind, the bow's limb tips could hit a side of the blind. As a test, draw your bow – with broadhead-tipped arrow in place – and swing it from window to window.

It would be nice to check out these details before you buy a blind, but that's probably not going to happen. Sit on your shooting chair at home, long before the hunt, and have a helper make some measurements for straight ahead, left and right shots. This will give you the information you need to buy a large enough blind, and, of course, if you're uncertain, err on the high side.

LIGHT DRAW BOWS

A ground blind is great for young hunters. You can sit in the blind with a youngster and help coach him or her through the whole process, reassuring them and giving them confidence. A blind also will hide the inevitable fidgeting a young hunter will make. Crossbows are often used by young hunters; a ground blind can be an added aid to help them be successful.

Hunting from a ground blind gives an archer a level shot, an opportunity to shoot side to side through the bear in the bottom third of its body. There will be no heavy bone structure to shoot through, as there would be when shooting from a tree stand. By shooting at the bottom one-third of the bear, you have a much better chance for a pass-through arrow and a quick, heavy blood trail. This is the perfect set-p for lighter draw weight bows.

SETUP AND TAKEDOWN

Blinds need to be set up and taken down quietly and quickly, so choose a blind that is light and has a carrying case for easy transportation. The less noise you make and the faster you get it done the easier it will be to leave the area undisturbed.

Always set up the blind when you go to hunt. Just be sure to allow enough time to set up the blind, get into your blind and get set, with enough time to let the area cool down from your disturbance.

If you bait and stay there to hunt, put a sealable cover on the bait bucket and stash it in the blind. If the thought of that makes you uncomfortable, hang the pail, unsealed, in a nearby tree in such a position that a bear standing to check it out will open itself up for a good heart/lung shot.

I believe bears have a fear of man up to a point. In a situation like this, I believe they leave the blind alone when they know you are there because they do not fear you and you make no threatening moves. If you press an issue with them, things will change. This is why I emphasize you do not need to fear a bear, just respect it.

They have no problem, however, returning at night and ripping to shreds a blind left in place.

Important: Always … repeat, always …take the blind with you every time you are done hunting for the day. Bears may destroy the blind when you are not there, as shown in the accompanying photograph. Taking it down at night, then setting it up again the next time you hunt that bait is extra work but well worth it. Blind replacement can get expensive.

SCENT CONTROL
Always make sure you are as scent free as possible when hunting from a ground blind. Shower in unscented soap, wash your cloths in unscented detergent, and before you walk into the blind spray yourself head to foot with a scent-neutralizing/covering spray.

At the set-up location, erect the blind and spray the exterior. Once inside the blind, spray yourself again, and spray the inside of the blind.

ATTRACTANT SCENT
Spray you favorite scent attractant on brush and trees in the space between the blind and the bait. Do this every time you go into the bait, whether it is to bait or hunt. Freshening the bait site tells the bear that you have brought supper and it is time to eat.

I like to use aromatic scents because they are effective everywhere and legal everywhere. Anise oil, liquid smoke and bacon scent are the best. Bacon grease is good, too, but it is not legal everywhere.

SCOUTING
When looking for a place to hunt from a ground blind, the most important thing is to be sure you can approach the blind without disturbing the area. Never cross the bait to get to the blind.

The area you want to hunt should have water or damp cover close by, and thick cover close to the bait. Bear will feel secure, and they like to get out of sight fast when they expect danger.

Be sure, too, there is brush and small trees to place your blind in or near. The less noticeable the blind the better.

Go to Chapter 5 – SCOUTING – for additional information.

BAITING
Go to Chapter 6 – BAITING & SCENTS – for details.

BAIT SET UP
Go to Chapter 6 – BAITING & SCENTS – for details.

HUNTING WITH A LEAFY/SHAGGY SUIT, BUT NO BLIND
At first blush, you may wonder if this is just a little bit more excitement than you want. But why not do it? It can be a rush, one heck of a thrill and greatly satisfying when you pull it off. All sorts of challenges lie ahead - overall nervous control, hunting skill, self-control at the moment of truth, the thrill of being "down in amongst them" so to speak, with an animal that could be dangerous but would much rather flee.

Taking advantage of the mobility you can have in a bear hunt of this style can be the difference between success and failure. You can move if the wind

Photos: Sandy Wiesner

• *For ultimate excitement, sit on the ground without a blind. Wear a shaggy or ghillie suit, set up so your outline is even more broken and you can come to full draw with minimal movement, then get comfortable and wait.*

changes, or if bears approach from an unplanned-for direction and you need to adapt before the next one walks in.

Your approach to your seat of choice can be from any direction the terrain and wind direction allow. Always approach into the wind.

How it began…

I first tried this system as an experiment to see what the results of different set-ups would be. I tried calling a bear to a decoy in one instance and watching an ordinary bait in another. A scent container hung over the decoy. My main effort was to see if a bear would come to a breeding sow moan and a challenge call.

I learned that, when cold calling (not over bait), you do not know where the bear will come from, so you need to take all precautions when doing this and be able to see 360 degrees. I also learned that control of human scent is very important, so now in this setting I use scent-free soap for clothes, take a bath or shower using scent-free soap, and use scent-free spray on my clothes, boots, hat, gloves…everything…upon setting up.

One time I called when a young bear was sniffing the decoy and the sow-in-heat scent on it. I used the challenge call and he just about turned inside out. He came within inches of running over me. I figured I was onto something.

When I first started doing this, I did not film. I was doing this to see what different setups would produce. I got camera equipment when things got to a point I felt there was a method to pass on. First thing I learned then is that the camera has a start up noise, but if you turn it on and set it on standby it is silent.

Gear and on-site prep:

• You need minimum cover, which is good because you want to change as little vegetation as possible. Create places you can sit in front of or behind brush to break your outline and hide your movement as you lift bow or firearm to shoot. Do not make a big pile of brush in an effort to be better hidden. A big bear will notice the change. Big bears don't like changes, so

Hunting Style

keep things as natural as possible.

• At the same time you select and prepare the bait site, prepare three or four spots to sit. You do NOT want to be changing any part of the area after bears begin coming to the bait. Get it all done at once so the bears can become accustomed to the single change at each site. These positions to sit are selected so you can hunt that bait no matter the wind direction. NEVER walk past your bait to get to your stand. This is very important.

• Carry a small clippers to trim only the brush necessary to create a shooting lane, and not one tree branch more. Set up for a left- or right-handed shot, depending upon the shooter(s) who will sit this bait, to minimize movement at the moment of truth.

• If you can find ambush locations that will let you have a tree at your back and a semi-circle of brush in front of you, you will have a good setup. The tree will hide your outline, and you can lean against it so your back doesn't get tired while you wait.

• At the same time, always be sure you can shoot in any direction without interference from whatever brush you positioned in front of and beside you. This will have you better prepared for any surprise.

• Make note of what the sun's location and path will be while you'll be on stand, for two reasons: 1) You don't want reflection off any of your gear or clothing or glasses or watch; 2) you do not want to be looking into a low sun at an approaching or feeding bear. This can be an important factor because you're on the ground, not up in a treestand looking down at your target.

• You need to sit so your bow or gun will be pointing directly at the bait at all times. You will be positioned to shoot with minimum amount of movement, and that movement will be vertical, which is less noticeable than horizontal movement.

• If gun hunting, you can sit on a pad on the ground. The pad will keep you warmer by preventing heat loss to the ground, and you will be more comfortable. Turkey hunters use a hinged seat-and-back pad with straps on the sides to hold the back upright. This is more comfortable than just a ground pad.

• With a bow, use a small, collapsible, portable chair of whatever seat height works best for you. An 18-inch chair will work well for most hunters. Be sure you can make the shot with minimal movement and no noise. Test your chair at home. Lean hard in all directions, and turn in all directions as you lean. If the chair is going to squeak, it will squeak during this test.

• Use face paint to avoid the restriction of a mask; a mask also can distort your sight picture.

You will be in close quarters, so be sure everything on you and on your hunting arm will be silent when you move to shoot.

• Bring along a sealable bladder jug. You may be there a long time, and you don't want to move any more than absolutely necessary.

The moment of truth...

When a bear appears DO NOT move on it. Take a deep breath. Try to get your shaking under control. (Don't tell us you won't be shaking. This is peak self-imposed tension time.)

Wait until the bear settles down at the bait and its attention is on feeding.

Then shoot.

Watch where the bear runs. Be specific in your observation and mentally mark the spot it ran out of sight by noting a tree or shrub or other easily identifiable marker. You're on the same plane as the bear, so the perspective will be more difficult, compared to being in a treestand.

With a well-placed shot, the bear will fall within sight or you will hear the death moan if it ran out of sight. Be aware, though, that not all bears make the sound.

BLACK BEAR ANATOMY & SHOT PLACEMENT

Quick, clean kills should be every hunter's goal. A broadside shot within your confident shooting range should make that happen. Broadside is best because it offers the largest view of the vitals, an arrow or bullet has least body mass to pass through before hitting the vitals and leaves the most room for error while still being quickly effective.

• The best shot is broadside, and the best target is the heart/lungs vital area. Wait for the bear to move its near front leg forward, exposing the vitals.

• Bullet or broadhead goes straight through on a broadside shot and should create entry AND exit holes. Aim 1/3 to ½ the way up from the bottom of the body. As you're picking THE SPOT, be aware that a bear's hair is long and makes its body look larger than it is. On a quartering away shot, aim for the desired exit hole and adjust entry hole backward as needed.

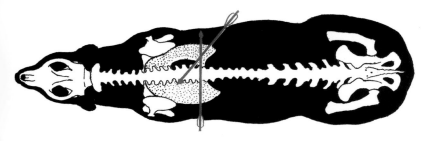

The Black Bear

The more you know about the bear's body structure, the more fascinating you will find this big game animal, and the better should be your skills in placing broadhead or bullet where it will do the most good the fastest. Our thanks to the National Bowhunter Education Foundation for allowing us to reprint these educational illustrations.

Skeleton

Illustrations courtesy of National Bowhunter Education Foundation
Go to www.nbef.org to order a bear-info packet

Black Bear Anatomy & Shot Placement

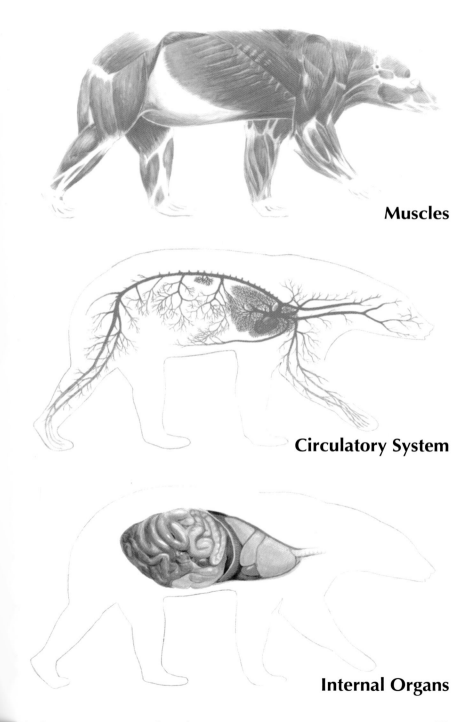

Muscles

Circulatory System

Internal Organs

"NOT Even the Cows......"

It seemed fitting to have a wild foods dinner the night before leaving for a spring bear hunt. Getting in the spirit of things, and all that.

So Judy prepared a bear roast, dandelion salad and rhubarb kuchen (a German custard-based dessert), and said, "Ok, guys, dig in."

The guys were Byron Ferguson and Larry Bauman. Byron is the archery trick shot artist you see on cable television regularly and at Deer & Turkey Expos in the Midwest and Mid-South, and a long-time friend. Larry is an excellent bowhunter and long-time friend from Missouri.

Neither Byron nor Larry had had any of those foods before. Rhubarb -- pie plant -- doesn't even grow in the South.

The feasting started out tentative but picked up considerably after the first couple of bites. Roasted bear meat and rhubarb kuchen disappeared easily, but the dandelion salad needed a bit of promotion.

"Dandelion greens have been eaten for ages," Judy noted. "They're edible only in the spring when they're still young and tender, so they're sort of a spring tonic. With hot bacon dressing, dandelion salad is just like endive and spinach salad."

"You're sure....?"

"Yes, I'm sure. Try it."

"Here you are, Larry." From Byron.

"No, that's ok, Byron. You have the salad bowl right there in your hand."

Much of this was for show...or was it? Didn't matter, because they dug in and liked it. At least, they said they did.

It must have worked. Later that week, we each arrowed a bear. Larry's bear scored 20-9/16 and for a time was the ninth largest black bear in Pope and Young Club's records. It weighed 355 pounds dressed.

Back home after the hunt, Byron told his father about the hunt and also described, in detail, the wild game meal at our house.

Byron's dad looked at him a minute, then said, a large dose of incredulousness in his voice, "Son, not even the cows eat dandelions!"

He had no comment on the rhubarb.

WILTED SALAD

In a one-quart dish of torn greens (dandelions, lettuce, spinach, endive or escarole) add 1 Tbsp salt, a dash of fresh ground pepper and two chopped green onions.

Fry 4 slices of cut up bacon until crisp and remove from heat. Add 1/4 cup white vinegar and 2 Tbsp water and pour hot dressing over salad. Toss. Serves 6.

RHUBARB KUCHEN

| 1/2 C shortening | 1/4 C sugar | 1 egg yolk | 1-1/4 C flour |

Mix shortening and sugar together. Add egg yolk and mix. Add flour and mix. Moisten with a little milk until dough looks like pie crust. Pat dough into bottom and up the sides of a 10" x 14" pan.

Cook 4 cups diced rhubarb in 1/4 cup water until tender. Spread rhubarb in the crust and sprinkle with 2-4 Tbsp sugar.

Custard: 2 eggs plus 1 egg white, beaten   3/4 C sugar   1/2 C milk

Mix all ingredients and pour over rhubarb. Bake in 350 degree oven for about 45 minutes or until custard is firm. Serves 10-12.

Reprinted from **THE WILD PANTRY** *published by Target Communications.*

80

CHAPTER 5 - *Memoir*
ONE-UP...AND ONE DOWN

As a bear hunting guide, I took only bow hunters and never had a problem filling my schedule. However, one year a rifle-using big game hunter from Michigan's lower peninsula called. He was determined to hunt with me even though I told him I did not take gun hunters. He offered double the price of a bowhunt; that made the decision to accept him much easier.

One evening while other hunters in camp and I sat around the campfire telling 100 percent true hunting stories, in pulled a new pickup truck and out stepped a portly gentleman. As he walked up, we all noticed he was dressed like he had just stepped out of a Cabela's catalog.

He joined us at fireside and as stories were told by other hunters in camp, he always added a bigger and better one.

He was soon nicknamed ONE-UP and referred to as such in our conversations when he wasn't around.

Here's why:

• One hunter said he had hunted the Big 5 in Africa. One-Up said he had done that twice.

• Another hunter mentioned he once killed a whitetail at more than 500 yards. One-Up commented that he shot one at more than 1,000 yards with a custom bull-barreled .375 Magnum.

• A third hunter mentioned he had been hired by his state's DNR to help eliminate coyotes in the urban area where he lived. One-Up said he had been commissioned by an African government to kill a rogue lion.

As the fireside story-telling ended, One-Up stayed back to ask a question. " What do you do if a bear tries to climb your tree?"

Without missing a beat, I told him everyone knows you sprinkle pepper around the base of your tree. He acknowledged my reply and walked away.

Soon after this...real soon...I talked to one of the hunters in camp, explained what happened and suggested he bring up the bear-climbing-your-tree topic at the pre-hunt meeting coming up.

Later that evening at the introductory here's-what-to-do-and-don't-do meeting, we went over judging bear size, when to shoot and not shoot, shot placement, what to do if you hit a bear and things of this nature. Then came the set-up question:. "Does anyone know how to prevent a bear from climbing your tree?"

One-Up's hand went up immediately. "Everyone knows you put pepper around the base of the tree."

Gotcha!

As a couple of days passed, hunters were seeing bear and taking bear, all except One-Up. So one night I followed him to his stand, made sure he was in place and left. An hour before dark, right at the perfect time to shoot a bear, I came back to make a from-the-road check. As I approached his truck I could see him sitting in the truck munching on a snack. Rather upset, I held my cool and told him that if he wanted to tag a bear he needed to sit until dark.

His explanation was that he wanted to eat a sandwich before prime time. It already was prime time. Who knows the real reason he was sitting in his truck at that time.

When he came back to camp, suitably after dark, he told us he had heard the dominant bear, not just a bear, circling his bait but never saw it so had no shot. He must have had great hearing and great vision and been clairvoyant regarding the pecking order of bears in that area.

The next night at dark he drove right past our cabin, where we were to meet, drove to his cabin, grabbed his gear and was gone. We never saw him or heard from him again. He hunted two nights. There's a strong chance he was afraid of bears.

People react differently to bears. They can bring grown men to their knees, so to speak.

• One hunter carried his bow, a .44 Magnum pistol and a .300 Winchester Magnum rifle, just in case. He could have held off an army of bears with that firepower.

• Two brothers always hunted together. They stood back to back on one stand so no bear could sneak up on them.

• Another hunter would wait to get out of his stand until he saw the beam of my flashlight as I approached on the trail to his stand. He stood in the dark a long time, because I had seven hunters to pick up over a 75-mile course, and he was the last one.

• A friend told me about a hunter he saw coming out of the woods after dark. That hunter's flashlight beam never hit the trail he walked on, but it did hit all the places he thought a bear might be waiting off the trail, ready to pounce.

• Another outfitter/guide told me about a client who would wait on stand until he saw the headlights of the truck coming to pick him up. Then he would climb down from his stand, run down the trail from his stand to the road, then stand in some bushes and wait. As the truck pulled up, he would saunter out of the bushes acting nonchalant.

"Kinda difficult looking nonchalant when your tongue is hanging to your knees," the outfitter told me.

CHAPTER 5 - How-To
SCOUTING

Before you can do any scouting, you have to know two things:
- **Where black bears live**
- **What black bears eat**

HABITAT DETAILS

First, put yourself in the bear's paws – heavy black coat of thick under-fur and outer hair that holds heat. The larger the bear the less comfortable it is in the heat.

Then, do some speed scouting. It's a good way to begin any scouting. You cover a lot of area quickly and look for tendencies. In large areas you know are bear country, drive around and look for places bear would like to call home from spring through fall:

• Cool, low, thick areas (cedar, spruce, alder, or willow swamps), plus creeks and river bottoms with weeds and long grass and tangled brush alongside them. Bears do not like open areas but will go into those that provide food, such as crop fields in the East and Midwest to open range in

Two types of bear country. Lots of conifers, heavy brush, swamps and water.

some areas of the West, if they can quickly get to and from cover.

• A little open water here and there in areas without flowing water.

• Ridges and slopes nearby with a good availability of natural foods, such as berries, acorns and nuts of various kinds, depending on the time of year, plus, in agricultural areas, corn and oats. Some places, such as hazelnut thickets, do double duty as food source and security cover.

You now have a great starting point from which to begin finding the details of specific areas that hold bears. It is a matter of checking for, and noting, the necessary details.

As you check, keep this point in mind: A bear is a solitary animal. It socializes with other bear but does not mix well with other species.

RUNWAYS, TRACKS & SCAT

Scat, tracks and runways are good starting points.

Runways

• Travel corridors get bears from secure areas to water to food and back to cover again, and to find mates during breeding season. Tracks in the runway and width of the runway will tell you deer trail from bear trail. A bear trail may be 12 inches wide. Bears break off grasses in a wider area than do deer and often travel in areas not conducive to deer movement. There will be times you cannot differentiate between the two.

• *Claw marks of a good-sized bear, made as it braced its front paws against this spruce to lick bacon grease scent attractant that had been smeared on the tree.*

Photo: Glenn Helgeland

Once you locate a bear travel corridor, try to determine direction of travel When you determine where they are headed or coming from you will know how best to locate your bait and stand, because it gives you a better idea o where to place a stand to ensure daytime appearances. Bear travel corridor are not as consistent as whitetail travel corridors.

You will be in the general bait area; pinpoint accuracy for stand placemen on the bear's approach isn't as important as positioning a deer stand. You know exactly where the bear is headed – to the bait. You don't always know wher a whitetail is headed.

Always think of the bear's stomach. Finding enough food is the mai

• Look for front foot tracks; they will be wide and short and toe pads will show clearly in soft terrain. It would be nice if the tracks were this size, too.

Photo: Bill/Sandy Wiesner

objective most of the year, including when your hunt begins. If it is the breeding season, you shouldn't mind having females at your bait. A shooter male will find them and won't run them off the bait.

Big bears normally find an area they like and take it over, running off other bears. When you have a bait with only one runway coming into and leaving, one size scat and one size track, this is normally a big bear bait site. Of course, trail cameras would verify that.

Bear Tracks and Trails

Bears often leave indistinct tracks (toes and/or claws not showing) unless they walk through soft mud or snow, because they walk on the soles of their feet. The front foot's small round heel pad seldom registers. There are five toes on each foot. They tend to toe-in, especially with the front feet. Front tracks are wide and squarish; rear tracks are longer. The rear foot, including the heel, registers.

They often walk with their rear foot falling slightly in front of where the front foot fell. The entire impression made by both feet creates a double track every once in a while, leading to reports of huge track sizes. In deep snow, bears direct-register by placing their rear foot in the same hole created by the front foot.

Any bear making a five-inch-wide front paw track is a shooter bear, but that's not a hard-and-fast rule. Females have smaller feet, in proportion to body size, than do males. In northern Wisconsin about 15 years ago, I shot a 300-pound female with four-inch front pads and another person in our party shot a male with four-inch footpads but weighing only 200 pounds.

Bears make their own trails, but also follow deer trails and forest roads. A true bear trail through grass may be close to 12 inches wide, with all grass matted down or a series of depressions created by many bears placing their feet in the same footsteps.

Trails approaching favorite marking trees often look different because bears frequently stomp their feet as they approach the tree. They twist and slide each foot, scent marking each track.

There should be a dance named for this.

Scat & Droppings

When bears are eating only fruit, nuts, acorns or vegetation, their scat does not have an unpleasant smell, having, instead, a slightly fermented version of whatever the bear ate. Scat containing meat or garbage smells somewhat like you would expect it to smell, but nothing as intense as animals that eat more meat.

When examining scat, in addition to noting the odor, look for seeds, leaf fragments, insect parts, hairs, bone fragments, scales, and such. If it is large diameter, it is a good bear. Latex gloves come in handy here. Find the living sources of these clues (fruit trees, berry patchs, oaks, etc.) and you're much closer to pin-pointing bait site and stand locations.

Your examination will be more successful if you have previously studied to learn details of vein patterns in leaves, the appearances of different kinds of seeds, hairs and insects.

Individual scats generally weigh one-half to one pound and will be tubular, loose or watery. Loose or watery scat means the bear is eating moist, soft foods (berries and tender plants). Scat from meat may be watery.

Photo: Glenn Helgeland

Photo: Bill Sandy Wiesner

• *Big coils of scat mean a big bear. For perspective, note the two quarters to the right of the scat.*

• *Some bait foods give bears diarrhea. The bear that left this pile had been eating granola flavored with molasses.*

Hunting tip: If a bear is hitting your bait at night, bring in dung from another bait and place it at the first bait. This evidence of an apparent intruder means competition; the first bear may now come in before dark to check out the new situation.

EVALUATE SIGN

Size of scat indicates size of bear. Only large scat at bait means a big bear took over the bait; lots of scat of medium or small size means a number of average to small bears are hitting the bait.

• Rubs on trees is a marking post or they are scratching themselves. If they are scratching, it will be only three to four feet off the ground. A marking post is made as high as they can reach and is more well defined through the bark to the sap wood. If scratches are vertical it may also mean a young bear is climbing because of danger from other bears or humans.

• When multiple bears are hitting the bait, front paw tracks in the frye grease and sand you will have spread around the bait should tell you what you have.

Scouting

TWO TYPES OF FOOD SOURCE

There are two types of food sources – natural foods and the bait you set at a site.

Set bait sites near natural food sources, but do not compromise your stand locations by trying to get too close to natural food. Being in the same general area is close enough and works well. Too close will cause too much disturbance when you set up and in your approaches, presence and departures from the stand.

Check natural food sources for bear sign. If bears are feeding in such an area now (four to six weeks before season), it will not be good when season opens. Look for foods that have not yet ripened but will do so as season opens.

I receive calls every year asking why active baits suddenly shut down. Simple...natural food sources have become ripe and are productive. Once corn and acorn crops are ready, bears switch to these natural food sources. You can't beat the real thing. When you can't beat them, join them.

Spring Scouting:

• Look for berries that ripen in the spring, grasses and soft mast.

• Locate possible stand sites or areas that also may be suitable for calling and spot-and-stalk.

• Determine into-the-wind approaches that do not cross the bait area and won't spook bear.

• Straddled trees and bushes are intense bear activity areas during mating season.

Males and females communicate by leaving scent. Both sexes leave scent by straddling saplings and bushes, urinating on the vegetation as they walk over it. I have heard they do this spring, summer and fall but have noticed it only in the spring before and during mating season. Sapling leaves will be torn or creased. When the straddling was done after spring green-up, the creases may be brown. Straddling and marking happens time after time along regular travel corridors. Tree branches may be bent or broken. There may be hair caught in the breaks.

• Look for marking posts, bite marks and claw marks on trees. All usually are signs of a good bear. A big bear often rubs a tree, leaving its scent to ward off potential intruders. Bite and claw marks are other messages of dominance.

Fall Scouting

• Look for nuts, acorns, other hard mast and corn. Scout the same for rifle and bow.

• Look for broken branches caused by bears feeding on plum, apple, chokecherry and cherry.

• Determine into-the-wind approaches that do not cross the bait area and won't spook bear.

Scouting Aids

Trail cameras are a big assist to fryer grease and sand when you're trying

Scouting

to identify the size of any bear, but especially when you intend to call. Calling is challenging a bear for its area. You're wasting your time if you call without pre-hunt preparation because you may not know if there's a good bear in the area.

BAIT & STAND LOCATION

When you have found good bear cover and food sources, located travel corridors to and from both, it is time to look at possible stand sites. Here are some considerations:

• Look for an elevation in the terrain and set up there. The height will disperse your scent better than in a low area and give you a better observation point.

• The protection of thick cover will offer security to the bear. It will feel comfortable coming to the bait earlier.

•Bears like apples. Apple trees like this are good places to begin a bait. Since they are accustomed to feeding here on their own, setting a bait here usually shortens the time until bears begin hitting the bait.

Photo: Glenn Helgeland

• Detail in the bait itself helps. Since bears will eat almost anything, your job is to put food in front of them that they prefer over nature's best. Try different things. I am always experimenting, trying to develop the ultimate bait.

• If you are in an area that does not allow baiting, spray attractant scents on ridges near ripened mast crops.

Distance From Road

On private property where no one else is allowed, you can go anywhere sensible. On public land, you may need to go farther into the woods because of road presence and amount of traffic on the road. Check size and condition of small lanes and two-track trails leading from main roads. Look for discernible vehicle and foot traffic on them. If there is none, you may be in business.

The main thing is that you do not start a competition with other bait hunters. You may find it helpful to check at campgrounds and resorts in the general area for the presence of other bear hunters.

STAND SET-UP

• As always, approach into the wind. Masking scents and carbon-impregnated clothing and scent-free showering are great, but why take a chance. If possible/practical, have stands at a bait suitable for approach under each wind direction. Approach quietly and directly. Do not walk through any area where a bear may be bedded.

• NEVER have the stand set up so you have to cross the bait to get to your stand.

• Set stand sites where bear come from swamps to ridges to feed. Don't get too far from swamp edges; bears will wait until dark to go into more open areas closer to ridge tops.

• If you will hunt from an elevated platform, go up the tree one foot for every three feet between tree and bait to set the stand.

• Be aware of positioning needs of right-hand and left-hand shooters, so it will not be necessary to turn for the shot.

• Some people like to stand, others prefer to sit, others do both so their legs and feet don't get tired and so they are standing for maximum body flexibility when the witching hour nears. Whatever your preference, locate the stand in an advantageous position to execute the shot and clear only the necessary branches.

• Be sure to hook up to a safety harness and be sure to have tried the harness prior to the hunt to be sure you have silent freedom of movement.

WINTER SCOUTING

These are things that can be looked at in the winter and used to help locate your spring or fall bait sites.

• This can be work, especially in north country with snow covering the ground. You can see more detail in a bare woods, but you'll be looking at coniferous areas, too. To check details, you will be walking and dealing with the cold, maybe snowshoeing.

• Look for territory that would hold a bear. (All the terrain and cover items mentioned earlier in this chapter.) You are not looking for dens.

• Check out places that appear to have potential. There will not be tracks, scat or other obvious sign, but you may locate a dominant bear rub on a tree, old broken off berry bushes, or hair on the bark of trees. Mark those areas well when you leave because when winter leaves, so does the look of each of the areas. After winter, as soon as the snow leaves (assuming there is snow), put out feeler baits to see if there are any interested bears in the vicinity. NOTE: Be sure to bait only when it is legal.

Photos: Bill Wiesner

• *Different views of top quality bear country.*

CHAPTER 6 - *Memoir*
AMBER'S DREAM HUNT

In 2011, a good friend of my son Bryan drew a bear tag for Wisconsin's Zone B. He could not make the hunt, so the tag was turned over to 13-year-old Amber Kolstad, the daughter of our very special friends Scott and Candi Kolstad.

Amber had been through all sorts of health issues. She was only two years old when she was diagnosed with leukemia. She was in and out of the hospital for treatments for four years. At the age of seven, doctors tried an experimental drug to control the leukemia, but she had several strokes as a result of the treatments. After the last stroke, she went into a coma and was given last rites two times. When she was eight years old, her spine developed scoliosis; if not taken care of, the pressure on her lungs, liver and heart would have killed her.

After all this, she wanted only to be a bear hunter like her dad and Uncle (in name only) Bill – me.

Amber doesn't like talking about her issues. She wants to be known as a bear hunter. And that she is! But everyone needs to fully understand the physical challenges she faced, her determination, her hard work in preparation for the hunt - in sum, her dedication. So we will talk for her.

Ten Point provided a crossbow. Easton provided crossbow bolts. Gander Mountain provided camo clothing.

Amber began practicing in June for the September hunt. Amber and her family live only three miles from us. Amber would come to our house three or four times a week and shoot for an hour. We helped her practice, with her shooting from her chair and using shooting sticks to hold the crossbow steadier. Her dad cocked the crossbow for her.

We had set up a hunt with an outfitter in northern Wisconsin who hunted with baits and with dogs. Amber would get the chance to experience both.

The first evening she sat in a ground blind with her dad. Bryan sat in a tree behind the blind and filmed Amber and her dad approaching the blind and getting into it. From his perch, he could get the bait and the blind into the viewfinder together. Should Amber get a shot, Bryan could get the bear's approach, presence at the blind, see the arrow come out of the blind (in

Photos: Bill/Sandy Wiesner

• *Upper left, Amber practiced all summer. Upper right, checking a road for a fresh bear track. Left, Amber in position on her chair, being handed her crossbow for the shot. Below, Amber and her father Scott with Amber's bear.*

Amber's Dream Hunt

slow motion setting) and hit the bear. That was the plan, and everyone was ready. The only thing needed was a shootable bear. No bear came to the bait that night.

Back at headquarters, we asked, "Amber, would you like to try hound hunting tomorrow morning?"

"Yep," she replied, grinning, without hesitation. That response was understandable. A ground blind sit with no action can get old quickly, particularly for a young hunter.

At 3 am, I got up to get a cup of coffee while Bryan began getting ready for the day's hunt. I stepped out of the hotel room and there stood Amber in the hallway, camo from head to toe and crossbow in hand. She obviously was wired. She and her parents roomed across the hall from us.

We were to leave at 3:30 to check baits, hoping one or maybe more had been hit. If more than one, we would check track sizes and decide which bear to put the dogs on at daylight.

We chased bear that morning but had nothing close enough for Amber to get to. At lunch, we asked "Do you want to continue to dog hunt again or sit a stand tonight?"

"Dogs," she said., with no hesitation.

That afternoon the dogs treed a large male, but the bear was back in the timber and Amber could not get to it. Another hunter in camp tagged that bear.

The next morning she was ready to go and we began checking baits at 6 am, same as the day before. We spotted where a bear crossed the road.

"There," a hound man said. "That's a big track. Get ready, Amber, this might be the one."

Dogs were released and the hunt was on.

Within 30 minutes we heard the dogs barking 'jumped', a different sound and cadence from their 'treed' bark. The jumped bark is more deliberate and drawn out. Two hours later the fast, choppy bark told us the bear was treed. Fortunately, the bear treed a short distance away, just off a two-track road.

Our group followed the hound men to the tree, with Amber riding on Bryan's back and Scott carrying her crossbow, shooting stick and chair. Bryan and Scott coached her on the trail in, telling her what to expect at the tree, with hounds barking and jumping around, guys getting dogs leashed, and the bear in the tree being the center of everyone else's attention.

Amber took it all in, watching the dogs' excitement, clearly enjoying their barking and focus, and the hound men working to leash their dogs to get them safely back away from the tree with the bear in it. No one wanted a less-than-dead bear falling in the middle of a pack of hounds.

While all this was occurring, her dad, Scott, worked to determine the best shot angle for Amber, talking to her nonstop to help her know what to do and keep her as calm as could be under the circumstances. She looked at various parts of this noisy, ever-changing scene, and kept looking back to Scott for reassurance.

Scott positioned Amber's chair and she settled in while Bryan cocked the crossbow, put the shooting sticks in place and handed the bow to her when she was comfortable.

"When do I get to shoot?," she asked.

"When we get the go-ahead from the head guide," Scott replied. That came an instant later.

"Ready, Amber?," the head guide asked.

"I think so," she answered, looking first at him, then at Scott, then at the bear.

She made sure the bow was steady in the sticks and against her shoulder, aimed carefully for what seemed an eternity at the bear thirty feet up in a big spruce tree. Finally she had Scott take the safety off, exhaled as she had been taught for better aim and squeezed the trigger.

The arrow went through both of the bear's lungs. In a couple of seconds it began to slip, then lost grip and tumbled to the ground, a quick, clean kill and a stone dead bear.

Amber had her wish...and her bear.

We had tears in our eyes, all of us, hound men included. All involved had put special effort into months of preparation: baiting, shooting practice, talking about the hunt, and talking more about Amber's dream, her dedication and her preparations to be ready.

This was a story of true success, to have Amber overcome all the hardships in her life, to see Scott and Candi for years keep their faith. Amber became a bear hunter that day and gave us all a lifetime of memories

It is still very hard for me to get my mind and emotions around it all when I think of the problems and challenges that have taken place in Amber's life. Everything ... everything ... she does in her life is a challenge. She is very special.

CHAPTER 6 - *How-To*
BAITING

Where is baiting permitted?   What baits are permitted?   What is considered bait?

Each state and province has its own laws for baiting and the use of scents, with allowed and not-allowed products described in printed regulations and/or websites.   Some classify spray attractants as spray attractants and declare them legal. Others classify spray attractants as bait, making them illegal where baiting is not allowed. Definitions of meat and meat byproduct differ.   For instance, Wisconsin considers beaver castor a meat byproduct because it comes from the beaver's body, thus making it illegal. Meat cannot be used in Wisconsin.

There may be restrictions on the amount of bait that can be placed at a site, and/or specifications on the size container allowed and how/where that container can be placed, or whether it must be placed in a hole in the ground, or whether it must be fastened appropriately to prevent bears from taking it.

Use bait containers the state or province allows. Biodegradable containers may be required. Non-biodegradable containers, such as plastic, metal drums and plastic bags, may need to be removed after the season. Where containers are allowed, you may be required to remove all content, containers and any other refuse when done hunting.

Some jurisdictions require each bait site be labeled with the user's name and contact information.

Laws and regulations change. Be current with them.

Spring or Fall Hunt?
Spring
The trick to any successful bait is to keep the bears fed. Time of year dictates the bait to use.

I like to use bakery products, plus meat scraps where allowed. Granola is a good bait. Bears like it; it has great shelf life; it absorbs syrup, molasses and honey; it is easy to mix and carry.

Other good baits that have served me well:
- Dried bread with fryer grease or molasses poured on it.
- Sweets of any kind.
- Gummy bears, licorice and oats with fryer grease added.
- I have heard dog food and other commercial products, most likely enhanced with fryer grease or molasses, is good bait.
- Popped popcorn works well. Bears love it, but it doesn't stay with them long. They're soon back for more. Popcorn becomes ineffective in the fall when a bear is feeding heavily on foods that have nutritional value.

Fall
- Natural foods – berries, nuts, soft mast, hard mast, corn, oats.

Photo: Bill/Sandy Wiesner

Photo: Mike Brust

- *Trail camera photo of a good bear leaving a bait it really liked. Bait in a hollow log will make any bear work, which should give an on-site hunter a chance for a good shot.*

- *The marks near the bear's left ear are cake frosting, appealing to the bear's sweet tooth. The frosting is seven-and-a-half feet off the ground. This is a huge black bear.*

There is one food item – chocolate – to stay away from. Its use as a bait item is banned in some states and restricted in others because it causes heart failure in animals. Chocolate contains theobromine, an alkaloid found naturally in chocolate. Theobromine exists in different levels in various types of chocolate and is most intense, of course, in blocks of chocolate. Baker's chocolate and dark chocolates have the most theobromine; milder chocolates have the least. Small amounts, such as found on the surface of some baked snacks, should be ok; that type of baked goodie has been used for baits a long time. However, there are better ways to appeal to a bear's sweet tooth.

Honey burns also are illegal in some places.

On the other hand, one scent item – **peanut butter** – fortunately is ok to use. That's great, because it is fun to smear on a log or a tree and watch bears try to dislodge it when it sticks to their tongue, gums and roof of their mouth.

Bait Site Separation
How far apart should baits be set up? Good question, but better to have

• *Peanut butter is a good scent bait, smeared on a log or tree trunk. Watching a bear try to dislodge peanut butter stuck in its mouth is entertaining.*

Photo: Glenn Helgeland

them a good distance apart than too near each other. I try to keep them several miles apart, hoping this keeps bears from getting the scent of my other baits and thus having only one or two bears hitting my entire bait line.

During mating season, with males travelling everywhere, this may be problematic. However, many males will be travelling, so several may visit any or all of the baits. It's not much different from the deer rut.

• BAITING with an outfitter

I send a sweaty old shirt in a sealed plastic bag to the outfitter when he is getting ready to begin baiting. He will bait every day, and he hangs my shirt where my stand will be. As the hunt approaches, the bear or bears relate the guide's scent to feeding time. The bear becomes accustomed to my odor as well as the guide's. Once I arrive in bear camp, I have the outfitter take me to my bait. From that point on, I take care of baiting. If my scent suddenly appeared as a new factor, bears hitting the bait would have been alarmed.

Simple steps like this aid in your success as a bear hunter. Assistance you provide the outfitter only improves your chance for success.

A few days before the hunt, I call the outfitter for an update on bait activity. It is always nice to get into the hunt mentally prior to leaving for the actual hunt.

A serious mistake hunters make is to ask to be moved if they do not see a bear right away. The only time you should ask to be moved is when the bait stops being hit or is being hit only by a sow with cubs.

I once did a study over a couple years. The results were interesting. Bait-hitting success rates on a six-day hunt were as follows:

- Day 1   5%
- Day 2   10%
- Day 3   15%
- Day 4   20%
- Day 5   25%
- Day 6   25%

I believe this increase was because bear related my scent with being fed, with that feeding accompanied every day by a familiar human scent that meant food to them. Normally, when bears are active, you DECREASE the amount of bait to build competition over the food, which will bring them in earlier. Big bears will take over a bait, pushing out smaller bears because of lack of food.

As you can see, patience is important when pursuing black bears. The bottom line here is that every time you ask to be moved you, in effect, establish a new bait. A couple of moves like that and before you know it you have run out of time.

Remember, you are paying an outfitter for his service and for what he knows. Listen to him and your success will be more likely.

• BAITING on your own

Start baits as early as possible, a month prior to your hunt would be great. Bear will use the security of darkness to come to a bait until they feel comfortable coming in during daylight hours.

If you can't bait as often or as early as you wish, look for someone living in the area you plan to hunt and see if you can strike a deal. You provide bait and bait containers; the local person does the baiting. If you do not know anyone or cannot find anyone to help, run a small ad in a local newspaper and offer to pay.

If this doesn't produce, you have no choice – bait as early and as regularly as you can and hope for the best. For daily baiting, arrive at least a couple of days early if you can; three or four days ahead would be even better.

In the 1990s in Ontario spring bear hunting, the publisher's father and a fishing buddy made it a practice to go into camp four days early to fish and set bear baits. He would take over the baiting from his father when he arrived, and he and the hunting partners who came with him always had active baits to hunt the first night. They didn't know the size or number of bears hitting the baits, but something is a lot better than nothing, and it was exciting finding out.

Starting baits early gives you the opportunity to determine whether anything about the bait needs adjustment. Bears, especially mature bears, don't like changes. A dramatic change may cause such a bear to abort the bait site.

• Start with a small amount of bait, unless you have used the bait site in the past. An established bait site is proven territory. As soon as bears in the area get a whiff of your bait's aroma, they know exactly where to head.

I usually start with five gallons. I also am a firm believer in baiting often, with fresh bait, rather than placing large amounts of food at longer intervals. Baiting infrequently with large amounts of food accomplishes little. The bait becomes stale, moldy and unappealing to a bear. It also allows them to eat at any time of day or night, which you obviously don't want.

Years ago, I baited on weekends, with average success at best. So I went north and talked to people living near the area I wanted to bait, hoping to find someone I could trust who would be willing to bait for me more frequently than I could. I even ran a small ad in local newspapers. The ad worked.

It's a disadvantage having someone else's scent other than your own on bait sites. The only way to overcome that, to a degree, is by also baiting the stand yourself on weekends or whenever you can. Reliability of the person you hire can be a concern, too. No matter; I still prefer this method to baiting too much and infrequently.

Number of baits. A minimum of two baits per hunter is suggested. When

Baiting

you're trying to get baits started, do as many as you have time for to increase your chances of getting baits hit.

Bait middle of the day. Bait runs after work or later in the afternoon will condition a bear to become nocturnal, simply because its food is arriving late in the day. Baiting at mid-day allows the area to settle down. Bears will be more likely to move before dark.

Bait regularly. Dumping large amounts of bait and not baiting every day will keep the bear in a sporadic feeding pattern. You want bears coming to the bait before dark on a regular basis.

Sanding or Raking. Sand the perimeter of the bait or rake an 18-inch wide circle down to bare ground around the bait. Then pour used fryer grease on the sanded/raked area. Strain the grease before using it. In some states, grease may be illegal if pieces of french fries or deep fried chicken are in it. Straining eliminates that concern.

Greasing the area serves many purposes:

• A good paw print in the saturated ground gives you a solid clue to the size of the bear.

• Prints of various sizes give you a good idea of the number of bears feasting on your bait.

• Bears take scent with them when they leave the bait, creating scented trails back into heavy cover and extending the attractiveness of your bait. Keeps your scent out of that area, too. With luck, more bears will be brought to the bait. More than one bear hitting a bait creates competition.

Make the bear work. Cover the bait with logs or rocks, slowing down the bear, making it move around to get at bait, and in the process offering a good shooting angle. This can be a 'V' of logs with shorter logs covering the bait, or longer logs laid parallel over the bait, or a barrel fastened in place.

The best bait cover we have seen was seven or eight dead spruce trees with trunks roughly 16-18 feet long and three inches in diameter, with all bark gone, branches broken to one-foot lengths and roots broken to one to two feet long. The trees were laid parallel, limbs to limbs and roots to roots, with the bait under the lower parts of the trunks, just ahead of the roots. The broken branches automatically interlocked when the trees were placed and thus became spring-loaded.

Bears needed to move the tree trunks to get at the bait in a hole beneath the trunks. One easy swat with a front paw would swing the top trunk out of the way, but as the bear reached for the second trunk to move it, the first trunk snapped back into place, hitting the bear a good lick. Bears did not like this, not at all. Three swats and three hits created an extremely frustrated and angry bear, getting louder and moving faster with each tree. This bait site was effective and highly entertaining.

• **Remain as scent free as possible.** A bear's nose is its best defense. Never set your bait in a place you will have to walk past to reach your stand. Have more than one approach, if practical, so you're good for various wind directions. Keep the number of people baiting the stand to a minimum; the fewer human scents at a bait site the better.

Good moves for all bear:
• Avoid too much contact with the area;
• Whenever possible, only one person baits the site.

• **Do not become upset** if a number of bears come to the bait at first. When a big bear comes to the site, it will chase the smaller bears out of the area and claim the bait as its own. If a big bear doesn't show up, there may be a shooter bear among those hitting the bait. The greased ground will tell you.

Sometimes, the more bears the merrier. More bears means more competition for the bait means a heightened urge to get there first means bears arriving at the bait during good shooting light. Key factor here, of course, will be one of those bears being of shooter size.

Scents & Lures

Bears will come to a number of attractant scents. The challenge is to decide what to do at a bait being set the first time. The trick is to figure out which attractants appeal to the most bear. This is either research or trial-and-error.

Beaver castor is the best bear attractant I have ever used. It is a pungent paste from glands on both sides of the beaver at the base of its tail. I remove the castor from each gland, mix it with mineral oil, soak cotton balls in it and hang the cotton balls near my bait. This is the only attractant I have found that brings bear no matter what the other contents of the bait.

Castor is available from commercial trapper supply houses if you don't want to prepare your own.

There are containers on the market with a wick and a sealable lid that work well in place of cotton balls.

When you use it, hang the cotton balls or container as high as possible so scent disburses to a larger area.

Photo: Glenn Helgeland

• *This bear would really like to get its paws on the scent bomb hanging from the pole below it.*

• *Freshening a beaver carcass scent attractant hung on a line out of reach of bears and high enough for breezes to spread its scent.*

On the more pleasantly aromatic side, anise oil, bacon scent and liqui smoke are the top attractants. Bacon grease is excellent, too, but its use not permitted in some states; artificial bacon scent works well in place of th real thing. These three scent products can be purchased from bear attractar manufacturers; anise oil and liquid smoke are available in grocery store These scents work well throughout North America.

Berry scents are effective, too, if used in the right locale. For instance, d

Baitin

• *Fish are not particularly good as an attractant; bears ignored these fish scraps so long the scraps dried up. The eight-inch hole in the barrel is a sizing tool for bear. If a bear cannot get its head in the hole, it's a shooter.*

Photo: Glenn Helgeland

not place raspberry scent in an area with no raspberries. On the other hand, there are exceptions to every rule, so try it if you wish.

In northern Manitoba a few years ago, ripe berries were everywhere. As a result, bears seldom came to baits and then only sometimes at night. I asked the outfitter if I could try beaver castor and got the go-ahead. We went to the bait an hour earlier that night and hung a few castor-saturated cotton balls. Two hours into the evening, a tap on my shoulder from my cameraman let me know we had a visitor. A nice male bear, about 275 pounds, was approaching the bait with its nose in the air. It walked directly to the cotton balls. The 15-yard broadside shot was made to order for my 50-pound longbow.

• You want the scent strongest at the time you want the bear to visit your bait site. That time, of course, is when you are there waiting for it. There is a way to make this happen.

When you begin baiting, spread a scented gel on trees around the bait. Do this every time you bait. After a period of time the bear will associate the freshening of the scent with its dinner arriving. Once you start to hunt the bait, hang above the bait a scent wick saturated with the liquid form of the same gel scent you put on trees. When you finish hunting for the evening, take the scent wick with you. This will condition the bear to come to the bait when you are there because the scent is strongest at that time.

• Not all experiments work. Years ago, I sat at a bait bears were pounding. Then everything stopped. The acorn crop had ripened and was heavy. Bears were gorging on them. I filled a pail with white oak acorns, poured them on the bait, climbed into my stand and sat there smiling in anticipation. The smile faded, then disappeared. Not only did bears not hit that bait, it sat idle the rest of the season. Go figure!

Liquid scent as main bait

On a wilderness hunt in Canada, the only bait I could use was what I could carry in with me. Liquid scent attractants were the only choice. I thought bacon, wild berry and shellfish scents would draw the most interest and put them in 32-ounce spray bottles. Shellfish was included because I was near a lot of water. Once I found fresh sign while scouting, I selectively sprayed the area. I had found a pond and applied the shellfish scent on bushes close to the pond to get good air drift.

I set up in the brush wearing my ghillie suit and waited. On the third day a nice bear came in, sniffing the air as it slowly walked, and I punched its ticket.

Using only liquid scents may prove less attractive to bears than traditional solid baits, but who am I to argue. This hunt was hugely satisfying. It pays to be adaptable, and to be prepared to be adaptable. It can open doors to a wider range of experiences on your hunts.

Liquid scents will be the main item where baiting is not legal, unless such scents would be considered baiting. Check the regulations where you will hunt.

Photo: Bill/Sandy Wiesner

• *Sandy and Nicole spraying attractant scent on a bear's marking tree at the bait.*

Setting the Bait the Right Way

A broadside shot is, by far, the preferred shot angle, with a quartering-away shot the only other sensible option. Head-on shots are acceptable only for centerfire rifles with the power to send a bullet through heavy bone protecting the bear's vitals, but even then this is not a preferred shot angle.

How to get the bear to stand sideways? For years, I built bunkers of wood and brush, trying to force the bear into a broadside position. However, the added brush at a bait site was an eyesore to the hunter and an alarm bell to the bear. Big bear will be extremely cautious approaching something that seems out of place. A low wall of logs, maybe 30 inches high so the bear won't climb over, tied to a couple of trees or posts on the far side of the bait might work. The logs would need to be long enough to prevent bears from reaching the bait at a 45-degree angle facing you.

A 'V' of logs used to be the standard setup, with the bait covered by short, heavy chunks of wood or in a five-gallon bucket. The bait would be inside the 'V' at the base, usually giving you a quartering away shot but also a broadside shot if the wings of the 'V' were wide enough.

If barrels are legal where you hunt, cut an eight-inch hole in the middle of an upright 55-gallon barrel, then chain the barrel to a tree in such a position that the hole is at a 90 degree angle to left or right of your stand. Fasten the barrel securely so no bear can move it. Put bait in the barrel through the hole, and sprinkle a bit of it atop the barrel for breezes to blow bait scent into nearby cover.

Jeff Brunn, a good friend and avid bear hunter, devised a neat, efficient way to force the bear to feed broadside.

Bury about 18 inches of a hollow stump in the ground at a 45-degree angle, then cut off the top of the stump parallel with the ground surface. It is nearly impossible for a bear to get bait out of the hollow stump unless it lines itself up with the angled stump pointing toward it. By placing the angle of the stump 90 degrees to your stand the bear will have to stand broadside to you to get at food in the buried stump.

• *A hollow stump buried in this position forces a feeding bear to stand in one place to get at the bait. Set properly, the bear will be broadside to your stand, which is exactly what you want.*

Ask a local logger if he has any hollow logs. A piece about three feet long works well. At the bait site, bury about one foot of the log in the ground at a 45-degree angle. Once the stump is in place, cut off the top parallel with the ground. This natural looking bait site also makes a bear more comfortable to move in and feed prior to dark. Make note of the various positions you may sit, to determine exact placement of the log.

There are other ways to go about this, too. A 'shotgun' metal pail, a piece of eight-inch or larger PVC pipe, or a five-gallon plastic bucket (painted black) will work. Any one of them could be buried at the proper angle. Cutting the bottom out of the two pails would allow drainage, should water get into the bucket, and keep the bait in better condition. All of them should be removed after the season; in fact, that may be a game law requirement.

You could simply dig a hole in the ground and put bait in the hole. Drawback here is that you won't have any control over positioning the bear for a good shot.

We use sweets, fryer grease and granola for bait placed in the stump.

One more step and you're ready to go. Rake an 18-inch-wide area around the bait. Saturate the bare area with old fryer grease to get paw prints and have bears spread the scent as they go back into security cover.

STAND PLACEMENT & SHOT DISTANCE

Determining the best place to put your stand at each bait site is a two-part decision – best place for bait and best place for stand in relation to bait location.

• What is your consistently effective, confident shot range? Place your ground blind or bow stand at that effective range, or less, from the bait.

• Bowhunting rule of thumb when shooting from an elevated stand: **one foot of height to one yard of distance from base of tree to bait**. If you have good branches and needles or leaves of tree cover, you do not need to be high in the tree. Most bow set-ups are for shots of 10-15 yards. To ensure hitting both lungs, apply this rule. You do not want to be too high because a bear is rather thick through the body. You want to get both lungs, and two holes are better than one.

• When shooting a firearm, you do not need to be as close, but there nothing wrong with it. Fifty yards is a good distance. Don't set up too far away. The longer the shot, the more bullet and vision obstructions there may be, and the more difficult it will be to pick an exact aiming spot in a vital area on the bear, especially in low light conditions. After a certain distance a bear is a black blob with no easily discernable aiming spot.

Do not be concerned about a long distance set-up to avoid alerting bear. In fact, from a longer distance you most likely will have fewer and poorer chances to see the bear as it approaches. If you cannot see the bear until it is on the bait, you may be inclined to rush the shot or not have a shot opportunity.

• If doing a D-I-Y hunt and you have not decided to use gun or bow, set your stand for the bow shot. You will be ready for handgun, bow, crossbow rifle, shotgun or muzzleloader use.

• If on a guided hunt, make your needs clear to the outfitter and do not let him try to talk you into something different. Be sure the stand is set for you, i.e., left hand or right hand shooting.

• Do as much clearing for shooting lanes as needed, but no more. Too much openness exposes you a bit and may alarm a bear.

• Pre-hunt erection of tree stands gives you time to check for unwanted noises. Spraying vegetable oil on a squeaky joint in the stand eliminates the noise. Small things like this reap large results.

SITTING COMFORT

Sitting at a bait can last hours, many hours. Discomfort leads to impatience and to shifting in an attempt to regain comfort. To prevent discomfort and movement at the wrong time, hang your stand before season and sit in it to be sure you can remain motionless for several hours.

A book to read helps pass the time comfortably. Small paperback books are easy to hold in your lap while you look up every half-page or so to check bait and surroundings. It is a neat feeling to see a black form silently moving into your peripheral vision as you read. Little movement is needed to slip small book into a pocket. Smartphones and texting among hunting partners is the current version of book reading.

Unnecessary movement may catch you in an awkward position when the bear arrives or the shot presents itself. A bear hunter I know showed me how to insert a piece of plywood between the tree and the butts of the metal rails underneath the platform so the stand feels level and insures comfort. couple of nails will hold the plywood in place. Remove them when you take down the stand. For whatever reason, our internal sense of balance makes a level treestand platform feel like it slopes down in front. The plywood fixes that.

Hunting Area Competition

Now that bear hunting is becoming more popular, the odds of having someone baiting in your area are increasing. In most cases your competition probably doesn't realize they are intruding on your area. Analyze your bait locations to see if they can be placed closer to heavy cover and entered without alarming bears. Whether moved or not, the only practical option is to try to out-bait the competition. Trying to locate the other hunters and decide territorial boundaries is difficult, at best.

You have a better chance during bear mating season. Continue to bait your present sites and hang a sow-in-heat attractant at the bait when you go in to sit the bait. Remove the attractant scent when you leave.

The interruption of a bait site in the fall requires more work to draw the bear to your bait site first. I backtrack an active bait to try to locate where bears are during their down time, before they get active and decide to feed. I then move my bait closer to that area and hope the bear will move past my location first.   I do this cautiously, because a bear crowded too closely may move out of the area.

TRICKING CAUTIOUS BEARS

There is no surefire method to bring in a bait-shy bear. The methods listed below can be successful or they can cause negative results, such as scaring off the bear or having it change its approach pattern to the bait.

They also may change the time the bear comes to a bait, making it difficult to decide when to hunt. That's the time to set up a trail camera, being certain that the time is set correctly on the camera.

If you have proof of a shooter bear on the bait you are hunting, and you know what you are after -- you have determined the bear's approximate size by tracks at the bait, in grease or sand, or from trail camera photos -- it is time to apply one or more of these methods.

•**2 in, 1 out**. Make enough noise when you and a helper approach the bait site to re-bait. You don't need to sing or shout or beat a stick on a tree trunk, but you don't need to be quiet either. There's a good chance the bear is lazing back in the bushes out of sight but well within hearing range. Sounds made as you bait can be great; the bear most likely already associates those sounds with food. As one person baits the site, the hunter quietly gets into the stand and settles in. Then, the person doing the baiting makes noises as he leaves.

• **Send one of your sweaty tee-shirts** to your outfitter so he can use it to spread your scent while baiting. Cut it into 6" x 6" squares, seal them into a sealable plastic bag borrowed from the kitchen cabinet. The outfitter can use these squares as drags when he baits your stands. The thought here is to have the bear associate your scent with the fact he is being fed by you. You do not want to smell up the area with your scent after the bear associates someone else's scent with the fact it is being fed. Your goal is to make it accept your scent, not run from it.

If the bear remains super-cautious, one way to defeat that caution is to leave a sweaty tee-shirt on the stand. Then, when you go in to hunt, put up a second stand as quietly as possible downwind of your existing stand and sit in that stand. The stand needs to be downwind of the bear's approach trail, too, of course.

• **Bring bear scat from another area** and place it near your bait. Try to place it so you will have a shot opportunity if/when a bear inspects it.

Plus -- May bring other bear to bait, dominant bear may check to see who is on his bait

Minus -- May spook bear off bait. Scent identification is big in a bear's life. Because of the strength of their nose they may identify the dung as from a bear they don't want to face.

They can judge another bear's size by the scent left at a bait. You generally can tell subordinate bears by their cautious approach, or hanging back and never approaching the bait. When a bear comes in with no hesitation, that's almost always the dominant bear on the bait.

• **Move your stand**. If a bear is scent-checking a bait, locate the route he is taking to scent check the area and set up downwind of that route. Determine as quickly and quietly as possible your new stand site -- and new approach route into the wind-- and as quickly and quietly as possible put up the stand. It may take a few days for results, so be patient.

Another option is to slip into the area and sit on the ground. You'll have to be downwind of the bear's approach trail, of course, and you will want to make some sort of blind to hide in or behind, or wear your ghillie suit.

• **Sow-in-heat scent**. On a spring hunt, place sow-in-heat scent on the bait site. Normally off to one side of the bait, in your effective range, and positioned so you have a shot.

• **Decoy and call**. In the spring, use a decoy with sow-in-heat scent with sow-in-heat call. In the fall, use regular bear urine and aggressive bear call.

• **Hunt at different times**. If the bear is on the bait at different times, play its game and hunt at different times. Use a trail camera to know the times and hours the bait is being hit. Otherwise, you're flying blind.

• **Take bait in and out**. Haul bait into stand when hunting and take it out when you leave. Place a small piece of bait at site when you leave just to let the bear know what it missed.

• **Change the feed at the bait**. Like humans, different bears like different foods.

• **Change the attractant scent** you are using or add more attractants.

CHAPTER 7 - *Memoir*
THE TOUGHEST MAN IN THE WOODS

When I moved to Michigan I met a guy who knew the woods inside and out and who, in that part of the Midwest, came close to being what is known as a Jackpine Savage, a label with no condescension but independence and respect and a bit of hermit about it all. He was Jacob Hill, an elderly gentleman who was downright ornery and not at all friendly at first.

I stopped at his house to ask if I could place a bear bait on his 120 acres of land.

"No bear huntin'," he growled.

I thanked him and left. In town, I talked to some people who knew him. They told me it would be wisest to stay away, that he was a bit cranky. No kidding.

It was obvious to me he didn't have a lot, other than an attitude and 120 acres of what looked to be good bear hunting territory. However, nothing ventured nothing gained. One evening Sandy cooked fish for supper. There were leftovers, so I asked her to make a plate for Jacob.

When I knocked on his door he answered through it, telling me the front door was not used, that I needed to go to the side door. I did. When he opened the door and before I could speak, he growled another "No bear huntin'."

Before he could shut the door I told him my family had fish for dinner and asked if he would like some. He said he would. He more than likely was tired of his own cooking.

This meeting opened a door to a friendship that would be tough to beat, and later to great bear hunting.

Jacob invited me into his home. I was amazed as I looked around. No running water; two small light bulbs for light.

He still made coffee on his wood stove in an open pan. He would dip water out of a bucket in the kitchen, place it in a pan, and when the water started to boil poured in the coffee. It would boil over every time. He once asked Sandy if she ever boiled over the coffee.

It got to the point that if I didn't stop every night after work he would be upset. We brought him a lot of meals, did his grocery shopping and did the paperwork to help him pay his bills. Some of the paperwork baffled him.

He told me he built his house by himself, digging the basement by hand. He had a sauna in his back yard. That is how he took a bath. He carried water from the Cranberry River behind his house.

I was helping Jake one day. We went into the basement for something. On the floor was a pile of deer antler sets, maybe 30 to 50 sets.

"Jake, did you shoot all those bucks?," I asked.

"You bet," he said.

"What was the biggest buck you ever shot?"

A big smile creased his face. He said he had shot a huge buck, one with massive rack and body size.

"Can I see those antlers?"

He smiled again and said he couldn't drag the buck so he went home and got one of his horses. As the horse was dragging the buck down the side of the road, a car pulled up.

"Where'd you get that buck?," the driver asked.

"On my property," Jake told him.

After some conversation, the guy asked, "You want to get rid of that deer?"

"Jacob looked me right in the eye and said 'I got two years free subscription to the FARMERS JOURNAL for that deer."

He laughed loud and long. To the day he died, he figured he put a good one over on that salesman.

I told him nothing different.

He told stories of his days as a lumberjack. Crews cut everything by hand with two-man crosscut saws. Crew bosses had to assign two men to work the opposite end of Jacob's saw. His strength must have been unbelievable.

Every time I stopped to talk to him, it was all about bear hunting. When he learned I used a bow he called me Bearcrazy Weisinger. He never did figure out how to pronounce my last name, and I never corrected him.

One summer afternoon he said he had a perfect place at the back of his property to hunt bear. Really! We walked to the spot, Jacob leading and me following. On the way, I noticed bear skulls alongside the trail. I didn't ask. We came to an area that at first sight I knew was one of the best bear hunting sites I had ever seen. It was a high ridge that dropped down to a thick swamp. The Cranberry River ran through the swamp.

The first night I was on stand, Jacob came to within sight of my stand at prime time and stopped.

"Hey!" he shouted.

I didn't answer because I didn't know what he wanted and because it was prime hunting time.

"Hey!" louder.

"What?" said just loud enough for him to hear me.

"You get down now and come in. Time to get out of the woods."

He didn't say what he was thinking, but I had to find out what he was thinking, so I climbed down.

"Come in now. It's not safe in the woods at dark," he said.

He didn't think I was safe because I carried only a bow. He thought I needed a firearm, too. (He always carried a double-bitted axe and a long hemp rope.)

I told him I'd always carry a .44 Magnum pistol on my bowhunts. That satisfied him and he stopped coming to get me at the magic hour.

That stand produced several bears a year for us for the three years we lived at White Pine.

Every bear we took off that magic stand had lead pellets in its rear end. Yep, Jacob would shoot them in the rear end when they came to his back yard to steal apples from his tree. He would open his basement door and give them one in the rear to chase them away.

Jacob had diabetes and went to a doctor to get checked. The doctor gave him medication that made Jake feel 'funny'.

"I think the doctors are trying to poison me," he told Sandy and me. He wasn't joking.

He had never gotten a driver's license. He decided to get one the second year we knew him. He had to go to Ontonagon to take the test. Sandy offered to drive him because she needed to go to Ontonagon, too.

The next day he stood by the road, wearing an old blue suit, waiting for Sandy.

When Sandy dropped him off at his home after he got his license, he said it was the first time a women had given him an automobile ride.

One day he was kind of in a playful spirit and asked, "How many swings will it take you to chop a four-inch diameter poplar."

"Two," I said. It took six.

Jacob found another tree about the same size and with two strokes of his axe, one left and one right, the tree fell, cleanly cut.

After three-and-a-half years of great friendship, one day I found Jacob passed away in his house. His death was unexpected. He had been in good health. The Wiesner family lost a true friend.

I was a pallbearer at his funeral, I was in my thirties; the next youngest pallbearer was in his eighties. At Jacob's funeral I talked to one of the other pallbearers. He worked in the woods his whole life and spent many days with Jacob. He told me Jacob started in a logging camp at the age of 15 as a cook's assistant. One day while he was emptying the garbage, a bear about 150 pounds startled Jacob. The bear charged and Jacob split its skull with a double-bitted axe.

"How did he get to the axe in time?"

"Jacob always carried an axe," the old gentleman said, by way of explanation.

Jacob was an amazing and interesting person, with woods knowledge like no one I ever met. I think of him often.

• *Byron Ferguson, famed archery trick shot, and an Ontario bear that scored 18-6/8.*

• *Wyoming bears DO know how to relax.*

CHAPTER 7 - How-To
NEW TWISTS & TRIALS

The hunting methods in this chapter – calling, decoying, food plots -- are much like decoying and rattling in deer hunting and work at about the same frequency. They are supports of the main effort; in bear hunting, the main effort is baiting. Decoying actually is a support of calling and of food plots. They are intertwined to a great degree. When they work, they can really be exciting.

• CALLING & DECOYING
Calling for bear began with the use of dying-rabbit sounds from a predator call. I believe that approach works better in the West than in the Midwest or East, simply because western bears do not have the abundance of food available to Upper Midwestern and Eastern bears. Several years ago, I called bears in New Mexico using predator calls. Those bears moved constantly, trying to find something to eat. Would you wear yourself out trying to beat others to a dying rabbit when there are 25 pounds of doughnuts readily available?

Basics of calling:

• Scouting is scouting. Look for high-percentage locations. As on any set-up, wind direction, time of day and possible intrusions are possibilities that will affect stand selection. **Go to Chapter 5 – SCOUTING – for details**.

• Set-ups can be on the ground or in a treestand. Best calling and decoying locations always will be tied to bait sites, for the obvious reasons. Hide in brush or use a ghillie suit (leafy or shaggy) to conceal yourself on the ground without obstructing a shot opportunity. If you don't want to sit on the ground, hang a treestand.

• After setting up, wait 20-30 minutes for the surroundings to settle down, including your scent.

• Call several times continuously for several minutes. Wait 10 minutes or a bit longer to see if a bear is responding. If not, call again. Continue to call until you see the bear or decide to move on. Bears apparently have a short attention span and will lose interest in your calling if you call just a few times. A bear will pinpoint your location, so be on high alert at all times once you start to call, and have gun or bow pointing at the bait. Your shooting window of opportunity will be narrow; you will have to be fully prepared and ready to act quickly. You may hear the bear coming before you see it. Take the first ethical shot the bear presents; it may be the only good shot you get.

Fawn Decoy & Calling Set-Up

When whitetail deer fawns are born, bears prey on them. They often follow pregnant does and eat the fawn the instant it drops. In many areas bears kill more fawns than do other predators.

The factor that separates calling deer from calling bear is that a bear is a predator and a deer is prey. To my mind, calling a predator is easier than calling prey. Pre-hunt preparation and set-up are 75 percent of success. When I started, I bought a fawn decoy and a fawn-in-distress call and proceeded with caution, concern and curiosity. Simulating the sounds of an animal a bear intends to eat puts the creator of those sounds in position to get injured, or worse

None of us can swivel our head all the way around, but in this set-up always make sure you have 360 degrees of view, a planned defense, and an escape route. You may see or hear a bear approaching, or you may not. I carry a pistol, not to shoot the bear but to fire into the ground in front of it should it charge, thinking I'm food. Hunting with a partner probably is the best, helping survey the area while calling. "Got my back" comes to mind.

Am I in harm's way when calling? I don't feel that I am. It is a matter of respecting the animal, knowing its behavioral habits, and planning and acting accordingly.

Photo: Sandy Wiesner

• **Bears prey on fawns in early summer, so a fawn decoy near a bear runway may work. I'm in my ghillie suit in the background.**

Timing for calling bears to a fawn decoy is important. Because spring bear hunts end in mid-June, when fawning is coming into high gear or is already there, hunt late in the season for best results.

For best results on any hunt, book your hunt for specific time periods that will offer the best opportunity to achieve specific goals, be that calling, baiting, guided hunt or spot-and-stalk.

I like to set up in hardwoods that border swamps. Newborn fawns lay up in grassy hardwoods, while bears like the protection and cool of the swamp. Female deer also like to hide fawns in grassy lowlands, such as on dry ground near creek banks and river banks. Trout fishermen see a lot of fawns.

Place the decoy in the open where a bear can see it easier -- a distressed fawn most likely won't be laying out of sight in the grass, but even if it is, the bear can hear it – then get set up and begin calling.

Cub Distress Call

I no longer use a cub distress call. Of all the calling techniques I have experimented with, I feel this is the most dangerous, by far. This method works in the spring when the bears come out of hibernation. The newborn cubs are easy prey for a big male and as gross as it sounds they will kill and eat the cubs. If a male bear finds the cubs and kills them, that sow will soon come into heat. The mom will defend her young ones but in most cases cannot ward off a big male.

If you want to try this, set up near a swamp where bears hang out in the spring. Call continuously for a few minutes, rest half an hour and, if nothing responds, try again.

Remember that treestand mentioned earlier....? It's safer.

Bear Decoy

Using a bear decoy and bear vocalizations is my favorite type of calling. It can work in the spring or fall by using seasonally-appropriate vocalizations with mouth call or electronic call.

Bear are vocal animals with a range of vocalization. The two to use are a female-in-heat moan in the spring and a dominant or challenge call for big males in the fall. Big males are continually on the move searching for a receptive female. The female moaning call starts lower, goes to higher pitch, then back down. The entire call lasts several seconds and should be repeated frequently.

My first encounter with a female in heat was memorable. I was hunting in northern Ontario the second week of June. A female about 150 pounds fed on the bait, then walked in long grass, moaning. She had not been on the bait long when a second bear appeared, than a third. I thought she was hurt or had brain damage. While she moaned, the other bears sparred and tried to approach her. She wasn't ready to be approached. Later, I realized what the sparring bears were trying to make happen. By nightfall I had seen eight bears. My goal is to replicate that scene when trying to call and decoy bears in the spring.

In the spring, make it a point to be in or on the very edge of the swamp. Long grass in the setup area helps. Females straddle the grass as they pass

• Hang a sow-in-heat scent wick above a bear decoy, then put it in a food plot or on the edge of the plot.

Photo: Sandy Wiesner

through, leaving their inviting estrous scent.

Get to the bait early and place the decoy in the area of the bait, but not right on the bait. I like to put the decoy in a position that trees or brush will be between the circling bear and the decoy. A decoy in the open may not fool a bear, but a decoy in the brush will. It's simply more natural.

The male will always attempt to confront the decoy face-to-face. Set up the decoy to be broadside to the bear when it first sees it. As it approaches a broadside decoy, it will begin to circle to come in head-on to the decoy.

There is little chance of the bear reaching the point where it will be exactly head-on to the decoy, because you should have a broadside shot before the bear gets to that point. Even if the bear is only five degrees to the side of being exactly head-on, it will see the whole decoy. A portable 3-D decoy would be great, but I don't believe one is made.

One huge early mistake I made was to spray the decoy with a synthetic sow-in-heat scent. Goodby, decoy! Now I hang a scent tube with a wick over a decoy; the tube is filled with synthetic sow-in-heat scent. Haven't lost any more decoys. I buy synthetic scent because it will always be the same, bottle to bottle. It is hard to believe companies can find real female estrus scent. How would they collect it?

Decide your set-up distance from the decoy according to the hunting arm you plan to use and whether you are on the ground or in a treestand. Hang estrous scent over the decoy and get into your stand. After the cooling down period, do several sow moans, wait 10 or so minutes and if there's no response, do another sequence of moans.

Stop sow moan calling at least one hour before dark. Males looking for love will be aggressive. If you are walking out of the woods as a male is coming in...

In the fall, use the more aggressive challenge call, something like saying "do do do do do do" through the call. There's no other way to describe it. The calling part is simple, locating a big enough bear to respond is the main challenge.

Once you start to see activity, pay close attention to the number of runways coming to the bait and size of the dung around the bait site. As noted elsewhere in other chapters, a dominant bear will take over a bait, chasing all other bears out of the area. This happens only in ideal locations. A big bear needs to have everything just right to want to claim an area as his own.

FOOD PLOTS

One of the questions that popped up frequently at bear hunting seminars I presented at hunting expos and in-store events was, "How do I keep bears OFF my deer food plots?" I began asking what they had planted. The main three were clover, turnips and buckwheat. This can be evaluated two ways – a huge dominance in acreage of these plants that limited the options for other plants, or an actual preference for them.

About 10 years ago, I got serious about it. Experimentation was fun and educational.

Food plots are big in deer hunting, but I don't believe they can be that strong in bear hunting. Food plots for bear are subordinate to bait. Food plots are not as attractive to bear as to deer, which is understandable since deer are herbivores and bears are omnivores. Ninety percent of a bear's diet will be vegetative, but it's not the same. Bears have a sweet tooth, which often is their downfall, and they like variety. They are opportunistic feeders.

However, a small food plot near or all the way around your bait can help in a couple of ways: 1) It offers the variety a bear likes, complementing the food items in a bait; 2) this smorgasbord can hold a bear on the general bait site longer than bait alone. I place my regular bait right in the middle of the food plot. Bears leave a bait if they're still hungry after the bait is cleaned up. Getting them back is nearly impossible.

One other reason for a food plot – baiting is illegal in some areas. A food plot, coupled with calling, may be your best chance. Liquid scent attractants may help.

Preparing and planting a food plot takes time and energy. You may not just be baiting bear but trying to out-bait other bear hunters, too. The extra goodie of a food plot added to regular bait can help here.

Step By Step

Since food plots supplement a regular bait site, the best food plot site will be on dry ground in open hardwood along a swamp edge, same place as the bait. Any food plot does much better when it can get adequate sunlight, thus the open hardwoods location.

A food plot 20 feet x 20 feet or near that size is large enough to be an attractant. If you don't have one, get a rototiller you can carry on your shoulder. A steel-tine rake works, too. The main thing is to break up sod -- there might not be any in a woodsy location -- and expose bare dirt.

Check a growing season zone chart before you buy seeds. The zones stretch east-west and tell you best planting times for each zone, varying by latitude. Many plastic seed bags have plant zone information printed on the back of the bag. Google has much information, too, probably more than you want or need.

Collect a soil sample and send it to a soil-testing lab. Expect to get the report in 10 days to two weeks. The report will tell you the amount of lime to apply, given in tons per acre. You will have to convert that to determine the number of pounds to spread on your plot. (There are 43,560 square feet in an acre and 2,000 pounds in a ton.) For a 20'x20' plot, one 50-pound bag should be plenty. Get pelleted lime; it is easy to handle and starts working its magic in the soil quickly. The report also will suggest a proper fertilizer strength and amount per acre.

While you're waiting for the report, spray the plot area with a Round Up-and-water mixture at the proper strength; 7-1/2 ounces per gallon is standard with concentrated Round Up. Do this a couple of weeks prior to seeding.

Photos: Bill/Sandy Wiesner

• *Spray a small area, around 20' x 20' feet, with Round Up, then rake it clean for planting.*

• *Sandy spraying the food plot area with liquid fertilizer prior to planting.*

Lime and fertilize before seeding and work them into the ground with a rake. This gives them a few days to begin working their magic.

Know when the plants you're seeding reach their peak of nutritive value. This will be the time they are tastiest for bear munching. Time your planting lead time accordingly. Use seeds that do not need to be planted deep, anywhere from being pressed into the soil surface to being covered by 1/8-inch of soil. You need only to break the ground to plant these seeds.

Plant the seed in mid-June to early July, depending on when you want the bear to find the spot. Most or all of the food plot vegetation should be ready at the same time you begin regular baiting.

Broadcast the seed with a hand-held seeder, available in any garden store or hardware store. Rake the food plot again to cover the seeds lightly. This helps seed germination and keeps turkeys from eating the seed.

Seed Combinations

There can be various good seed combinations, I'm sure. I have used a combination of buckwheat, clover and turnips, mixed equally by weight, that worked well. Buckwheat was the cover crop. This mixture offers something throughout the fall season. Clover and turnips did not reach maturity. The buckwheat did, and that's when the bear ate the seeds. Tenderness, which animals like, and the stage at which plants contain their highest percentage of digestible nutrients, are very important. Bears didn't eat turnip tops, but they began digging bulbs when the bulbs weren't much larger than a radish.

I check the progress of each food plot throughout its growing stages. This helps me document plant growth and see if the plot has drawn early-stage bear feeding activity. Normally, nothing happens in the food plot until regular bear baits are started. You may see early signs of bear activity in the food plot – plants nibbled and their tops bitten off, or a flattened spot where a bear rolled, or bear scat.

Bears will pound regular bait before touching the food plot. As time passes and the bear is content with his food source(s), it is likely to spend more time at the bait. At this time, expect to see areas of the food plot start to become utilized.

Secondary Benefit

The secondary benefit of a food plot comes into play if all regular bait is eaten before you re-bait. The food plot appears to be just enough to keep the bears' interest, and they spend more time in the baiting/plot area.

Make notes on what is happening at your bear food plot site(s). This tells you what to keep and what to change, including the plant species used.

In areas and states that allow food plots but do not allow baiting, this alternative may make the bear hunting success rate climb.

Photos: Bill/Sandy Wiesner

- **Bill top-dressing the growing food plot with more fertilizer.**

- **A lush food plot with a bait stump under the rocks filled with sweets and granola.**

Photos: Bill/Sandy Wiesner

- **A good-sized bear in a food plot.**

• Editor's note: The strangest bear bait I've ever seen...a knotted plastic garbage bag hung In a tree on the side of a road. The bag was not punctured, so no bait scent could escape.

• Norm Jolliffe crossing a Maine beaver dam to hang a bait bag on a bear runway near the dam.

Judging a Bear's Size

• Looks can be deceiving. The bear in the photos to the right looks to have good width, but notice how large its ears look compared to head size. This bear needs to grow a couple of years. For a better size evaluation, see its photo at the bait barrel in Chapter 8, page 128. The bear below has body depth, mass, proportionally smaller ears to head size and a squarer head.

Photos: Glenn Helgeland

CHAPTER 8 - *Memoir*
MEMORIES OF MICHIGAN & GARBAGE DUMPS

Years passed – 1971, when I got out of the service, until 1980 – and the hard work and years of bear hunting were beginning to pay off. I hunted and baited for myself and my family, and for friends, and was beginning to build a reputation – the right kind – in my home town, Sturgeon Bay. I had done exactly what I wanted and was beginning to get a really good understanding of black bears and black bear behavior... how cool was that.

In 1981 I was offered a job at a shipyard in Ontonagon, Michigan. It took me exactly one second to accept the offer. After all, now I was headed to the true north woods. We moved to White Pine, Michigan. The following two-plus years taught me a lot about bears, their habits and movement patterns – the habitat(s) and terrain they preferred, travel routes, where to find bears at different times of the year, how to judge a live bear's size, eating habits, what foods they liked and where to find those foods, at what stage of maturity or ripeness bears ate those foods.

My passion now turned to obsession.

My favorite pastime was to go to garbage dumps to study bear. But no one can do that any more, due to health regulations that require garbage be covered with dirt frequently. (I never saw a sick bear, though.)

Watching dump bears gave me a way to study their movements, listen to some vocalizations, and practice judging size. In a dump they would look at you briefly, then continue what they were doing. Dumps gave a false picture of their true wild nature and could create a dangerous situation if you misinterpreted that behavior. At a dump, you didn't get too close to them because they tended to defend their food.

I would spend hours, often daylight to dark, watching and documenting what I witnessed.

At the Bergland dump, garbage and non-food items would be dumped on a relatively high flat area, then pushed over the side of the dumping area. That left the top flat and clean. All the garbage would be in one sloped place, looking like a hillside. You could walk across the flat area right to the garbage -- if you wanted to. Bear would be scavenging the 'hillside' looking for food.

We always approached the garbage from the top of the flat. I would peek over the side to see where the bears were feeding. They could and would be anywhere from the bottom of the garbage hillside, about 20 yards below us, to the top of the garbage. We would see anywhere from no bears to 10 or 12.

• *Watching bears at dumps was informative and entertaining. Other people who came to dumps to watch bears were entertaining, too, always unintentionally.*

Photo: Bill Wiesner

The bears would briefly look up at us, then go back to feeding or searching for food. If one popped its teeth at us, we would back out and give it its space. When we encountered a sow with cubs, we gave them a lot of space. If they were close to the top of the garbage hillside, we left.

On occasion, friends would join us. One weekend a good friend came to White Pine to spend a few days with us. He and I had hunted together since we were twelve years old and still did on occasion. We planned a trip to the Bergland dump to see the bears, so guest, family and I piled into my old pickup truck and took the 15-minute journey south.

We parked about 200 yards from the dump's edge and quietly approached the dump.

My friend walked a few feet directly behind me as I carefully moved into position. About 10 feet from the spot I expected to see the bear, I stepped on a small piece of plywood. A rat ran out from underneath the plywood and right up my pants leg, fortunately on the outside. I screamed in surprise, and my friend was gone. He covered the distance to the truck in record time. That was his last trip to the dump.

The bears? When I screamed I ran back to the truck. My friend already was there. I don't know how the bears reacted to my scream; we were looking directly away from them and directly at the truck. Since there was only one scream and two fast exits, they couldn't see or hear any cause for alarm. They most likely looked up, saw nothing and went back to feeding.

Us? We went home and had a few beers. That rat was enough excitement for one evening.

****

On one weekend day in the summer of 1982 we had backed our truck into the spot we normally parked at the White Pine dump to watch bears.

We were just getting comfortable when a boat of a Cadillac pulled in. As the big car came to a stop, a door swung open and out stepped a man about six feet tall, 140 pounds, wearing Bermuda shorts and with a big ugly cigar in his mouth. He had a camera around his neck, so it was obvious what his intentions were.

His passengers were three young ladies who seemed to be impressed by this gentleman. They went through the chain link gate to get closer to the bear feeding on a bag of garbage.

We could see this turning bad quickly; anyone with bear knowledge could have seen it. I suggested he not approach the bear, that it could be dangerous. He simply waved me off.

Next he told the women to walk over and stand by the bear so he could take their picture. They started to do so, and the bear began to walk backward away from them, with its ears laid back.

I shouted to them again, with stronger language. (Totally unlike my normal self, of course.)

I no sooner had the words out of my mouth than the bear false-charged the women.

The man turned and raced for the fence. He jumped it in Olympic fashion, never missing a step and clearing it easily. The women were right behind him but went through the gate and dashed for the car. Doors snapped open and those four people appeared to be scrambling everywhere to get into the vehicle at the same time through whichever open door was closest.

Doors slammed...engine roared...auto backed...gears shifted...wheels spun...dirt flew from behind the wheels...and the big Caddy was gone, never to be seen again in that neck of the woods.

We enjoyed watching that exercise and always wondered what the women said to the guy on the way out of there.

****

I had taken a nice bear one evening and recruited family and friends to help track. Back then, the Coleman lantern, was the tracking light of choice. Put some aluminum foil in the back half of the glass and the light would reflect forward brilliantly, which really helped in tracking.

A neighbor, Don Revart, was always there when needed to help retrieve animals. His nickname was HI-FI because he was extremely high strung.

On one particular tracking session, Hi-Fi was on his hands and knees with the lantern, looking for blood. As he crawled under a spruce tree, a grouse flew out. Thinking it was the bear, he let out a yell like that area had never heard! He was 10 feet up that spruce tree in an instant; all reaction, no thought needed.

Instances like this will always be remembered any time bear hunting stories are told.

For us, it always has been a family thing.

My wife Sandy is an avid outdoor person. The first game animal she killed was a bear, and she did it with a bow on a hunt in Michigan. The Darton SL-50 was her hunting arm of choice. Its draw weight was 47 pounds, enough to kill any bear. She shot two-blade cut-on-contact broadheads. She shoots through most bear with this setup.

Taking that bear fired her passion for archery, and I now had a bear hunting partner for life. That first bear weighed about 175 pounds dressed and at that point was heavier than any bear I had taken.

Since then she has taken two Booners (21-3/16 and 20-11/16 score) and

Photos: Bill Wiesner

• *Memories of living in a cabin in Michigan's Upper Peninsula are all good. Our boys had friends to shoot with and play on monkey bars, and we had a constant stream of friends, clients and neighbors visiting. Yet we could be alone as a family when we wanted to be.*

two bears over 500 pounds. Both Boone & Crockett-class bears were taken over baits on fall hunts in Ontario, one in 2001 and one in 2003. We filmed both hunts. The outfitter used popped popcorn as bait. It was surprisingly effective. The outfitter has a stadium popcorn popper that popped a 50-pound bag at a time. He hauled the popped corn in a large bladder on the back of his truck.

She has made her mark in our little family world of bear hunters.

My oldest son Brad also broke the ice in Michigan when he was 15, shooting a 220-pound boar with a white blaze on its chest. The bear was dead in 30 yards. I captured it all on video to enjoy for a lifetime. Brad did the whole package: he helped bait, helped drag out the bear and skinned it out. Our entire family cut and wrapped the meat.

It is interesting how our family has measured our success in the outdoors by bear hunting efforts, bears taken, non-tagging experiences while hunting bears and simply enjoying seeing wild black bears be wild black bears. We had front row seats for all the activities. Many animals of various species have been taken by Wiesner bullets and arrows, but the conversation always centers around the black bear.

I cut my bear hunting teeth in Michigan's Upper Peninsula. I learned about baiting on my own. Trial and error showed me what worked and what

122   Memories of Michigan & Garbage Dumps

didn't, and from there I soon had an established, dependable way to bait bear. Every bait was set up to my specifications for stand placement, where to place the bait and how to place it to give the hunter the best opportunity for a high-percentage shot. At the same time I was able to fine tune proper shot placement, recovery of the animal and care of the trophy.

I had laid down the base of reliable, effective bear hunting methods from baiting to hunting to guiding , tracking and even bear meat as flavorful table fare, elements that, over the next 33 years as I continued to learn, would be tweaked and improved as needed.

Photo: Bill Wiesner

• **Leo Sarnowski was my bear hunting mentor. He was one of Wisconsin's early bow hunters; if he wasn't a charter member of the Wisconsin Bowhunters Association, he was close. He was soft spoken and a man of few words, but every word had meaning. He is shown here with my wife Sandy.**

Leo and I met in 1980 at an archery shop in Wild Rose, Wisconsin, his hometown.

He was retired as a self-employed carpenter and had time to hunt more and stay in camp longer. He would come to Michigan's Upper Peninsula, where my family and I lived at that time, to more or less hang out, help in camp and in the kitchen. He often arrived early and helped with baits before hunters arrived.

When I would select a place I thought would be good for a bait, he would ask why I chose that place. When I would set up a bait, he would ask why I chose to do it the way I did. He forced me to analyze and to think. Many times he agreed, other times he didn't. We talked in detail on everything I did. When he suggested a change, he would go into great detail on the reasons. I listened and learned.

He was an awesome cook, too. He frequently cooked meals when he came up for bear season. When he prepared a meal featuring bear meat, Sandy and/or I would write down his recipe and cooking tips. He also helped Sandy cook and wrap food to freeze for hunters' meals.

Memories of Michigan & Garbage Dumps

123

His bow shooting accuracy was amazing, and he often gave me shooting instructions. He taught me not to try and hold the pin motionless on the center of the target. Trying to freeze the pin there was trying too hard and made me shake. He suggested I float the pin a bit and relax. Because we both shot fingers, he showed me how to relax my fingers until the string slipped out of my hand, instead of jerking bent fingers off the string. That was a problem with a lot of finger shooters.

****

EDITOR'S NOTE: In high school, a couple of times I took dates to dumps to watch bears feed in the headlights of my car. Girls sit close when scary bears are running loose right in front of you. Because of that I liked dump dates, but one time watching bears was more than enough for the girls. Subsequent dates (sometimes there weren't any) were more likely to be a movie. They probably didn't want to become bear hunters anyway.

CHAPTER 8 - How-To
THE SHOT – BEFORE, DURING, AFTER

BEFORE

Bow/Gun Clearance in a Treestand

Trim limb branches differently for compound bows than for recurves and longbows. The most common mistake here is trimming too high and not wide enough for traditional equipment. When a stick bow shooter draws his/her bow, the bow is canted for the shot. This is a process of leaning the bow 25-45 degrees from perpendicular. This changes the geometry of the stick bow, making it about the same length as a compound, but much wider.

It also makes a difference if you are standing or sitting to shoot. Trim only the branches necessary to make the shot. Removing too much background leaves an 'open hole' effect.

Hang your rifle by the sling on a hook so you can reach and lift it with minimal movement. If you do not have a sling, lay the gun on your lap.

Put a bow hook or hanger in place, positioned so you move very little to lift the bow.

Practice draws sitting & standing, down left and down right, leaning against your safety harness.

Bow/Gun Clearance in a Ground blind

For bow shooting from a ground blind, it is a question of not only top and bottom limb clearance, but also side to side. The bow must be clear of all walls when you draw and shoot. The muzzle of a firearm must not touch the blind as it is lifted, because it will scrape upon contact. The less movement the better when it is time to shoot.

Do not ready yourself for the shot while the bear approaches the bait. It s on full alert.

Do not attempt to shoulder your gun or lift your bow until the bear is preoccupied, feeding on the bait. Make all movements slow and deliberate.

• Conifers – check pitch leaks on the tree. Figure out a way to keep pitch off your jacket and gloves. If there is a bit of hang-up, and you're not aware of it, there may be a tiny bit of noise when you move to get ready to shoot. Conifer bark can be noisy, too, without pitch. Get rid of the loose, noisy pieces of bark by scraping them off with the back of your knife blade.

Study the Bear (see four-color center section of this book)

• Study the bear skeleton, muscles, internal organs, and circulatory system. Learn bone structure and internal organ structure, and their locations. Be able to visualize them when you're looking at a black, hairy target.

• Notice that bear ribs are narrower and thicker than deer ribs. There's more space between ribs, and they do not get thinner near the tips.. A cross-section of a bear rib resembles a half-moon.

• A bear's shoulder blade is much thicker than a deer's shoulder blade. Do NOT try to run an arrow through a bear's shoulder blade; that's simply asking for trouble. A bear's shoulder blade is thicker near the edge than in the center of the big flat part of the blade.

• Learn where to aim on various shot angles, from tree stands at various heights and from ground blinds.

READING A BEAR'S BODY LANGUAGE

Approaching the Bait: when a bear approaches a bait, it is on full alert. There may be larger or more dominant bears in the area that have taken possession of the bait. Watch the bear closely.

Do not try to move into shooting position until the bear is preoccupied. Any premature movement will be caught and the hunt will end. Allow the bear to reach the bait and turn its attention to feeding. Then make your move slowly and wait for the perfect shot angle.

Being able to read bear body language enables you to understand better what might happen next. When a bear is looking around constantly or grabbing a mouthful of food and running off a short distance from the bait, there possibly is a bigger bear in the area or a female with cubs. Females are always defensive when they have youngsters. Pecking order among bears is always being established, and actions of the underdogs are always a good indicator of what the area holds. If the bear is not alarmed, it will return for more, and it will be more relaxed and more likely to remain on the bait and present the shot angle you want.

A spring bear feeding on natural food sources that walks through long grass could be a female in heat leaving its scent on the grass to attract a male companion.

A bear that licks its upper lip and nose is moistening its nose so the scent receptacles become more sensitive. It wants to get a better whiff of a scent it doesn't like or is curious about.

Sometimes a bear will enter a bait site and walk out without feeding or attempting to get near the bait. In the spring this can be a young male looking for a female while knowing a larger, more aggressive male nearby is looking for the same thing. This also could be a big male checking out the bait area for the same reason. The short breeding season finds males skipping meals to have more time to locate a girlfriend. And sometimes it simply is a pecking order thing with no breeding season urges involved. Bears can tell the size of a bear by the scent it leaves.

A bear hunting friend watched two hungry yearlings drop to their butts and stick their hind feet straight ahead to stop in time to avoid crossing the scent trail of a big bear that had crossed the bait an hour earlier. The young bears turned and ran back the way they came. The earlier bear had floated in like a black cloud, looked over its shoulder at my friend in his treestand, walked across the bait and out of sight, never slowing down or stopping and never offering a shot opportunity.

A dominant bear will mark a tree after it has chased away other bears hitting the bait. This is a common fall practice.

On a somewhat-related issue, watch as much of a full circle as you can. For two reasons:

• In the spring, when a female is hitting the bait, mature boars often will circle the bait out of shot range. They are checking out the situation. Your best solution here would be to set up another stand on the perimeter near where you have seen the bear, because more than one male will check things out. I have made this work a couple of times.

• Subordinate bears circle a bait more often than we see them doing so, but once in a while you will see a black head appear above some brush in heavy cover, then 10 or 15 minutes later pop up again 90 degrees from where you saw it the first time. It is simply being cautious, checking the wind for the scent of a bear larger than it is or any other scent that makes it cautious.

FIELD JUDGING BLACK BEARS

What to look for

• Adult males have a big head with a crease down the middle of the forehead (some females do, too); smaller cookie-sized ears in relation to head size; ears appear on side or 'corner' of head; thick, heavy front legs; body mass full and chest and stomach close to ground, and they walk with a rolling gait or a waddle.

• When the muzzle appears wide and short, that's a big bear.

• Differences between male and female: males have large heads in

• *A female will look short coupled and almost a round ball. This female had two cubs trailing behind.*

• *An immature bear's head will be long and slim, with ears appearing large in comparison to head size.*

Photos: Glenn Helgeland

• A bear that needs to stand on its hind legs to get a bite of bait atop a barrel needs to grow a few years.

• The back of a really good bear will be at or near the top of a 55-gallon barrel as the bear stands on all four feet looking balefully at the camera/hunter/treestand. Editor's Note: It knew I was there. I spent more than an hour moving around on my stand to see how the bear would react. The first 20 minutes or so it moved back into the brush about 15 feet. After that, it paid no attention to me. I didn't shoot it because I already had a bigger one on the wall. Another hunter in camp took it the next day.

comparison to females; a large female will have a head that looks small on its larger body; females have smaller front feet than males, seemingly out of proportion to body mass; females have shorter body length, almost seem as tall as long. Their overall body appearance is somewhat round. Males are longer-bodied.

Some sort of measuring stick at bait
• Light colored stick (white birch sapling, other light-toned stick, dowel rod) seven feet long, marked at five-foot and six-foot lengths w/ black tape, stick laid on ground near bait.
• Small pole tied horizontally at 30" or 36" near bait to judge height of bear standing on all four feet.
• Logs covering bait, five, six or seven feet long.
• Bait barrel, 55 gallons – Eight-inch hole in side between two creases. If the bear can't get its head in the hole, it's a shooter. On four feet, bear with back level with top of the barrel is a trophy; three-quarters up the side of the barrel is a good one, and a back halfway up the barrel is an average bear.

Other check points
• Triangulation -- width between ears, ears to nose. If all three sides are the same length, you're looking at a big bear. The smaller the bear, the shorter the line between ears in relation to lines from ears to nose.
• Big bears move more slowly, check their surroundings more often and more cautiously, seem to roll as they walk.
• Sexing – Male penis sheath hangs down. Female has pointed tuft of hair pointing down from the vulva, just below tail, often wet from urine.

DURING

SHOT PLACEMENT

Broadside shots always are best. Aim one-third of the way up the body behind the front leg. To make it even better, wait until the near front leg is forward, exposing the heart/lung vitals. The heart/lung region is the largest and best target. With guns, you can break a bear down by taking out the front shoulder with a heavy bullet. Their shoulders are muscular and shoulder blades are thick.

• On quartering shots, line up the shot by first selecting the spot you want broadhead or bullet to come out the exit side of the animal, then adjusting impact point of aim farther back so the arrow or bullet goes through the bear at the proper angle to come out at the proper point on the far side.

Photo: Bill/Sandy Wiesner

• This is where your broadhead or bullet should go with a broadside shot.

• If you're shooting from a treestand, keep in mind that from this overhead angle the bear's spine will appear to be closer to the middle of the body than the top. Aim lower to hit the vitals instead of big bones at the top of the body.

• You may want to consider a tracking string on your bow. Test the tracker prior to hunting. Some of today's bows are very high performance and tracker strings create poor arrow flight.

• Two holes are better than one.

Bear In Tree

Shooting up at a bear is an uncommon angle. Practice shooting upward at different angles.

AFTER

Tracking/trailing –

The noise of a gunshot and shock of a bullet/slug has an understandable effect on a bear. It has been my experience that a bear shot with a gun will bail out of a tree, but a bear hit with an arrow will climb higher. If a follow-up shot is necessary, take it quickly.

A well-hit bear generally drops quicker than a well-hit whitetail, but a poorly hit bear seemingly can go forever, right into the worst jungle or swamp you've ever struggled through.

A wounded black bear is one of the most difficult animals to track, for several reasons:

- Fat thickness can and does minimize blood loss. Fat can cover most or all of the bullet or broadhead entry hole, requiring considerable blood loss before there's enough to drop to the ground. A wounded bear can go a long way before that happens.

- Loose-fitting hide also moves the entry hole through the skin off the entry hole through everything under the skin, minimizing or completely blocking external blood loss. When a bear puts its near front leg forward, which is what you want, that loose hide is stretched. Once the bear is hit and runs, that loose hide slips over entrance and exit hole (assuming there is an exit hole), closing off a blood trail opportunity.

- Hair on a bear's coat generally is four inches in length. This, and the thick under-fur, will absorb great amounts of escaping blood from the wound channel before enough is built up to allow some to drop to the ground.

Different Trails

There are different ways to trail bear that have been shot with different types of equipment. I have seen a bear not lose a drop of blood from where it was hit to the point of recovery. With this in mind, it is very important to pay attention to everything the bear does after being hit.

After the shot watch closely as the bear runs away, if it can run away.

- Which direction did it run?
- Was it running with an odd gait?
- Where did it go out of sight exactly, not 'over there'.
- Did you hear anything once it was out of sight?

This information is important when making a plan to track the bear.

Fewer trackers are better than many; it's even better if they are experienced. A group of three seems to work best, with one on the trail and one to each side. Many times, because of the lack of sign, too many people will do more damage than good. The more helpers, the more excitement and loss of control.

Slow, deliberate movement is the rule. Trails are often invisible in swamps. Open water and moss disperse or absorb blood. Search carefully for every bit of sign; it may not always be blood. Tracks, broken brush, crushed grass and hair may take you to the next sign of blood.

Archery Hits

As a general rule, once you hit a bear with an arrow, give it plenty of time before beginning tracking. The exception to this, of course, is when the bear falls within sight or you hear the death moan, which are the bear's last few exhalations with vocal cords involved. It is a moaning sound that will make the hair on the back of your neck stand right up. Not every bear does this. Once you hear it, you won't forget it.

Most outfitters I have hunted with wait until morning to track a bear. Bear generally are black, and at night a black bear can present a problem. Outfitters normally carry a gun for back-up. You do not need to be moving around in the dark while someone with a gun is simultaneously looking for an animal that can be almost impossible to see and may not be where you hope it is and may still be strong enough to run away...or toward you.

A lady hunter we know did an after-dark trailing effort with her outfitter and a friend on a bear she shot just before dark. This was back in the days of recurve bows. Their flashlight beam was aimed at the ground for blood trailing. When they tipped up the flashlight to see what the trail led into, they saw two glowing eyes not 12 feet ahead. The eyes suddenly became a bear lunging at them. The lady threw her bow at the bear as she turned to run. After a short sprint, they realized the bear wasn't chasing them. Tiptoeing back to check things out, they discovered the bear's head had gone between bowstring and bow when the lady threw it and the bow acted like a very wide collar. The bear couldn't get between two trees, one on either side of the trail, and died there. The lunge was its last energy.

Firearms Hits

Normally, when you shoot a bear through the shoulders it will drop in its tracks. However, If the bear runs off, no matter where it was hit, wait a couple of hours, then proceed cautiously, searching slowly, carefully and patiently. There may be little blood even when the bear is shot through the vitals. A wounded bear will go through some nasty stuff...downed trees, water, thick brush, wet swamp. This is their home territory. They may go only fifty yards, but 50 yards in this type of bear woods is a long way.

Guided Hunts

What happens when you get a bear down? You get what you pay for. I have seen bear recovery effort/help from outfitters range from fully assisting the hunter to "you are on your own, buddy". To track a bear on your own in an area you are not familiar with is tough, at best.

I shot a bear on a guided hunt and returned to the lodge to tell the outfitter. His response was "Where's the bear?" I asked if he was going to help me get the animal. He told me he baited the bear, the rest was up to me.

Removing a bear from the woods is not a job for one person. I failed to clear this point with the outfitter prior to my hunt.

You will need to know, too, whether the outfitter provides any help once the bear is back in camp. Does he or one of his employees help take care of the meat to be sure it doesn't spoil? After a bear's internal organs are removed they have to be disposed of immediately. Whose responsibility is that? This is an area often overlooked.

Go to Chapter 9 – Hide & Meat Care – for details.

Dogs...the Best Tracking Aid

A trained dog is the best tool for tracking wounded bear, but only where use of a dog is legal. This is not a job for your house dog Fido. A trained dog will not get the handler or itself in trouble when confronting a wounded bear. The best trained dog I've seen is an Akita. Dogs of that breed are intelligent, have exceptional noses and are easy to control. A good dog serving the outfitter well shows everyone the outfitter's commitment to his clients and to the bears.

Other Tracking Aids

• There is a light commercially available that illuminates blood. Since wounded bears often leave a poor blood trail, this light can point out small specks of blood in hard to see places, such as moss and grass.

• Hydrogen peroxide makes blood foam. I carry a small squirt bottle of it and squirt a small shot on any spot that looks like blood but may not be.

• Pieces of reflective tape are used to mark last blood. They are easy to see in daylight and with a flashlight on night trailing. If you lose blood you can look back at the tape to determine the path the bear is taking. When the blood trail dries up, go back to last blood and work in circles starting small and gradually increasing the size. At times a bear will abruptly change directions. You need to find that directional turn.

• An older way that works well is to put aluminum foil in a Coleman lantern, with shiny side forward and foil tight against the glass on the back half of the glass. The shiny foil reflects light forward. Carry the lantern ahead of you, so you are behind the light and won't be blinded by it. With the light projecting forward ahead of you, you have an effective, efficient tracking aid with maximum visibility on your part.

Always, always take your time. Be patient and thorough. Do not ignore anything resembling blood trail sign, or any other sign you suspect the wounded bear may have created.

Grid Search the Area

When you absolutely cannot find sign, make a grid of small areas, about 50 feet by 50 feet, and check each area thoroughly for any sign -- a piece of turf the bear tuned up on the ground, a broken twig, hair, crushed grass. Tracking wounded bear is a challenge few, if any, other animals create.

If nothing works, check the area for water or extremely thick underbrush. Bear will head to these type of spots when they are injured.

Best Hunting Arm to Carry

A wounded bear at close range is something you need to be prepared for when tracking. Tracking bear always takes you to the worst terrain imaginable. The right gun is a consideration you can't overlook, something that can throw a lot of lead quickly at close range and hit what it is aimed at. A 12-gauge pump shotgun with an 18-inch barrel will do that. Put slugs in the tube and a round of buckshot in the chamber. This setup can be fired quickly, accurately and effectively, even from the hip.

• Using a stretcher or cot is the easiest way, by far, to take a bear out of the woods

Photo: Glenn Helgeland

Dragging Out a Bear

A dead bear has to be the worst animal to move. Even a smaller bear is like a bowl of jelly. The carcass will snag every possible thing in the woods. If you tie the bear's legs to a carrying stick and two or four guys rest it on their shoulders, tie the bear's body tight to the pole to keep it from swaying as you walk. Stretchers or cots, with a person on each corner, or three to a side for a really big bear, work much better and easier. If you are hunting on your own, recruit the help of a strong friend or skin and quarter the bear and pack it out. Check the local game laws regarding the legality of quartering a bear in the woods.

THE INFAMOUS "GROUND SHRINKAGE"

When estimating size and weight, black bears are the most misjudged big game animal in the woods. Bears simply look much bigger than they are, especially to hunters who have not seen several of them under the self-imposed stress condition of viewing one at close range with the intention of putting a tag on that bear. Therefore, the huge bear before the shot frequently becomes a much smaller bear when the hunter walks up to it.

Contrary to popular belief, all bears are not 500 pounds. As a matter of fact, a 500-pound bear is exceptional. Hair up to four inches long, often standing erect when the bear approaches the bait, adds considerably to the visible circumference of the animal. That, plus a bit of fear factor and general unfamiliarity with the animal, create large weight and size misjudgments

Over the years I have taken many first-time bear hunters to the north woods. Until that time, the only bear they had ever seen was at a zoo or in a picture. Not only did they tell me they wanted a 500-pound (or better) bear, when they shot a 200-pound bear they thought they had killed a 500-pounder.

In an Ontario camp one year, a father and his two sons were on their first bear hunt. I took a decent 200-pounder the first night out and after that contented myself fishing and visiting with the outfitter and his family. About six o'clock on the third evening an RCMP officer pulled into the lodge's driveway. One of the sons was so excited he had started to walk back to camp. The officer had picked him up on the highway.

The young hunter had a smile a mile wide and proceeded to explain his hunt. He said he shot a MONSTER bear climbing his tree. The outfitter asked "Where did you hit it?" "I don't know," the young man said, "but it died 50 feet from where I shot it."

I asked how big it was. "At least as big as your bear," he replied.

There was plenty of time to retrieve the bear before dark, so we headed out. On the drive to his stand, the young man explained how committed he was to bowhunting....thousands of hours of practice just for this hunt, etc., etc.

Parking the truck, we grabbed the cot to carry out the bear. The outfitter took his rifle, just in case. From the stand, we walked over to the young man's bear. The "monster" bear was a yearling, about 70 pounds. The young man's smile lit up the place. He was sure his bear was a trophy, and for him it was!

Later that evening in the lodge, he got into some Canadian whiskey and his mouth started spilling big stories that, after a while, were a bit irritating. Finally, he looked at me and asked, "What would you do with ole' big boy?"

"Tan its hide and make a wallet," I said. I probably should have apologized, but I didn't.

One year I tagged a 200-pound Michigan bear. A young lady at the gas station/convenience store came outside to register it, took one astonished look and said "Oh my gosh! That bear has to be 400 pounds!"

"Nope, sorry. It isn't more than 200 pounds."

"Nossir. It has to be 400 pounds."

"Why do you think so?"

"A guy registered a bear here 20 minutes ago. He said it weighed 250 pounds, and your bear is almost twice its size."

CHAPTER 9 - Memoir
NORTH TO CANADA

Michigan taught me the basics of do-it-yourself bear hunting. Now, by going to Canada, I began learning about bear hunting with a guide. Over the next several years I hunted with guides in several provinces of Canada. I learned that no two hunts are alike; you need to do your homework prior to every hunt.   Outfitters have to lay out hunts so they are sure to have everything needed to make their clients content with their hunt.

When I asked my second son Bryan what he wanted for a high school graduation present, his response was immediate. He wanted to go bear hunting. I was doing trade shows in the winter so we started our search for a guide that fit our budget and needs. After a lengthily process we found our destination in Sturgeon Lake, Ontario. It was a spring hunt, so we started to make our plans and prepare to venture north.

Preparation can be a learning experience in itself, as we found out. I do not know how many times we packed and unpacked, checking and rechecking to be sure we had all necessary items.

I sat with Bryan, video camera in hand, and recorded his first bear hunt. This was the time in my bear hunting career I began documenting everything on broadcast quality video. The time to quit my job, take out a loan for cameras and make bear hunting my full time job had arrived.   This step involved considerable thought and nervousness.

Our next trip to Ontario included my son Brad. We baited in a bear that played mind games with us. My camera stand was 45 yards to the side of the bait, high in an aspen tree. Every night when I climbed into my stand, I found a pile of digested food the bear had left on the platform. We tried every trick in the book. And after two weeks, one evening it walked into the bait early. It was our family's first color phase bear.

Several friends came to Ontario, many to take their first bear. They and we earned a ton. On anyone's first bear hunt, you're loaded with anticipation.

You soon learn that all the talk in the world cannot prepare you for the first bear hunting experience. The trip was as exciting as the hunt: crossing into Canada for the first time, exchanging money at the border, the different kinds of food at restaurants on the way up there, seeing a camp for the first time, realizing the size of the Canadian bush, sitting in the lodge at night talking about the day's hunt.

Plus things learned on the hunt itself: to always follow the outfitter's instructions to the letter; the extra excitement of tracking a wounded bear because it is a bear not a deer; the higher level of difficulty tracking a bear than a deer because bear blood trails almost always are more difficult to follow (lots of swamp, moss and water). We learned that stands can get better as the hunt progresses because bears become accustomed to your scent and know, too, that they're tougher than you are so they aren't all that concerned about your presence. We learned how difficult it is to drag a bear versus a deer.

Sometimes, too, it is more difficult picking an aiming spot on a bear than on a deer. This is more of a problem for gun hunters than bowhunters because they (gun hunters) usually are farther from the bait site than a bowhunter. The gun hunter will see more of a blob than well-defined shoulders and legs, particularly in low light conditions.

Then there are the misconceptions that quickly get corrected. Such as: the hours spent on stand are much longer for deer than bear (nope); how quietly a bear moves through the woods (to the point of total silence); that all bear don't weigh 500 pounds, and how to judge the size of a live bear to decide whether it is a shooter or not.

We met a Saskatchewan outfitter at an expo in Madison, Wisconsin, who invited Sandy and me to join him on a hunt at his camp. The drive from home was 31 hours, with the last five hours on a two-track road to his camp. We were 100 miles north of nowhere, a place the good Lord made specifically for hardcore bear hunters.

Transportation to and from baits was by boat. We always left camp early, around noon, so we could catch fish for dinner that night before going to our bait stands. Iced down, they kept well. That was fun. Fishing – excellent fishing -- often is a part of Canadian trips and shouldn't be overlooked.

I took a bear on that hunt with a left-handed bow Fred Bear hunted with. A business associate who previously was employed by Bear Archery in Michigan before starting his own business had received it from Fred and loaned it to me.

Our next stop was Manitoba…big bears and lots of them. On my first Manitoba hunt I saw more than 30 bears while alternating between three baits, tagging a nice black phase bear.

The trip to and from baits was long. We traveled by truck more than an hour to the top of a mountain range. Once we reached the top of the mountain, we unloaded the ATVs and ate lunch. It was at least another hour by ATV to the bait. Fun! We normally got to the stands around two o'clock and sat until dark, then made the two-hour trip back to base camp. Supper would be served at about 11 pm. Long days.

When you're hunting this far from camp, traveling by various means, you do not do your pre- hunt checking you could be in for a surprise. You're

Photo: Glenn Helgeland

• *Bear hunts often have great fishing, too, for walleyes and big northerns.*

Photo: Sandy Wiesner

• *Bill carried out this 175-pound Ontario bear because dragging it was more work and took too long.*

Photo: Glenn Helgeland

• *If you forgot it, you'll have to get along without it. Fly-in hunts and drives to the end of a road require careful, thorough planning.*

Photo: Bill Wiesner

• *Bryan and Nicole Wiesner, front, and Terry and Lorna Wood, rear. This was Nicole's first Canadian bear, taken on her and Bryan's honeymoon.*

Photo: Bill Wiesner

• *Sandy Wiesner with an Ontario bear that weighed 512 pounds and scored 21-9/16.*

not going back for something you forgot. This is important anywhere, but especially here. Since you're in Canada, you're also a long way from home and all the gear and clothing and boots and various necessary backups you may not have brought. Complete and accurate preparation is key. Make a checklist to help your prep.

Eastern Canadian bear hunting was a bit different, but not a lot. In 2010, Sandy and I and her brother Greg and his wife went to Quebec for an early spring hunt. Insects weren't a problem; they weren't out in force yet.

This hunt proved to be a good place to call bears, because our hunt was during their breeding season. We called in and saw two bears but got no shooting. We hadn't yet begun working with decoys; I believe they would have helped.

Unfortunately, our outfitter did not know much about bears. (Value of homework, remember, and the problems of not asking enough questions.) His was more of a moose hunting and fishing camp. For instance, he dumped only one two-pound coffee can of dog food per night at each bait. However, with that said, we saw bear every night and Sandy passed on a shooter bear we saw the night it was her turn to sit with the bow and my turn to film. We had words about that afterward.

It was a great lodge with great meals, and a good bear population in their territory. The only weakness was a lack of bear hunting knowledge. This hunt was a good example of the necessity of doing all your homework and contacting references, others who have hunted there.

Along that same line, a friend went on an outfitted hunt where the outfitter had his dog with him at all times. He let the dog run all over the baits while he baited them. He also must have reeked of dog smell, which may have lingered at the bait. I'm not sure how much of a negative this was, but it certainly couldn't have helped. Dogs and black bears aren't exactly best friends.

CHAPTER 9 - How-To
CARE OF MEAT & HIDE

BEFORE

FIELD DRESSING BASICS

Moisture and heat are the two worst enemies of wild game headed for the cook pot. This is especially true with bear, for their heavy coat and, maybe, heavy layer of fat just beneath the coat, will drastically slow down body heat loss. Bears, especially big bears, are heavily muscled too; larger muscles cool slower.

Don't be concerned if you have to wait until the following morning to track a bear hit the night before. We have never lost a bear we let lay overnight.

Also, DO NOT open a bear's body cavity to dress it if you have a long way to travel prior to skinning. Carry it out on an adapted cot or stretcher; you won't want to put rope marks around the neck or paws if the bear is a trophy. You will get out of the woods with a clean bear.

If you have to field dress the bear in the woods, do so as soon as possible, then keep the bear's body cavity dry (although it's advisable to wash the blood out first, then dry the cavity), and cool the carcass as much as possible as quickly as possible.

Quick cooling, and keeping the carcass cool, will prevent hair from slipping, among other benefits. This is vitally important when you plan to have a bearskin rug made or a mount of any kind.

Also, a good field-dressing job requires some knowledge of animal anatomy. More than one animal has been ruined because the hunter didn't realize there were such things – heart and lungs – ahead of the diaphragm that needed removing.

• Don't open the animal from end to end unless you can remove it easily and quickly from the field and plan to process it right away. Meat exposed to the elements begins to spoil immediately in warm and hot weather. Leave as much meat covered with skin as is possible until you get it out of the woods. It will remain fresher, if you take proper steps to cool it quickly.

• Once you have opened a small cut on the belly, cut from the inside as much as possible to avoid cutting hair. Loose hair sticks to meat. Also, a small opening pays dividends when an animal is dragged from the woods. Fewer sticks, leaves, grass, moss and dirt items can get into the cavity.

• Be careful not to puncture stomach, intestines or urinary bladder with your knife. If this accidentally happens, or the arrow or bullet already has done the puncturing, wash the intestinal cavity with water and dry the cavity immediately after washing.

• With a heart- or lung-shot animal, you may find it cleaner and easier to remove only body cavity contents behind the diaphragm in the field, then hang the animal heels up in camp to finish the job. Blood from the heart/lung cavity will drain down out of the chest cut you make to open up the carcass and will leave the remainder of the body cavity clean. This also will keep gastric juices in the esophagus from draining down into the body cavity.

• Remember that shattered bone acts like shrapnel and penetrates meat around the wound. Trim all this meat, even if it doesn't look bloodshot, and err on the heavy side, at least one-half inch.

EDITOR'S NOTE: We cooked and tested some meat near a wound that did not appear to be bloodshot. Not good. Tasted like rubber, although, since we've never cooked a tire, we can't be certain of the exact taste match.

Care of Meat and Hide

After you find the bear, it is up to you to take the necessary steps to insure that meat and hide are taken care of properly. The first and most important steps in this process happen long before the hunt.

1) Taxidermist

Be sure you have a good taxidermist lined up (check some of his previous work, on bears especially), and have a talk with him. Talk about the type of mount you may want. Ask him how and where he, the taxidermist, wants the bear hide cut so he can give you the best results. Ask him the 'what and where' of measurements he needs so he will be able to properly make your trophy look good and realistic. (Understand that, without knowing what the bear will measure, the taxidermist does not have an exact idea where to begin. So you will have to cover a handful of possibilities and 'what ifs'). A bear is difficult to duplicate and without proper measurements it is a nearly impossible job. Make complete notes now for later reference (a sketch would help, too). Remember to have a camera with you on your hunt. Remember to take quality photos of your trophy from several angles, to give to your taxidermist for reference and taxidermy accuracy.

On a hunt some years ago, the outfitter refused to follow my instructions on how I needed the bear skinned for the mount I planned to have done. After some back and forth, I told him as nicely as possible that he had done his job and now I needed to do my job correctly by following what my taxidermist needed.

I have had other outfitters tell me they have taken care of more bear hides than any taxidermist. Makes no difference. It is your trophy and it is up to you to insure it is properly taken care of. We're talking quality here, not number of bears skinned.

2) Outfitter

Most -- emphasis on 'most' -- outfitters have freezers for clients' game meat and hides. Check this in detail before leaving on your hunt so you will know what your outfitter has available. Find out exactly what he has, so you will know what you need to bring and what you won't need to bring. Then bring it anyway. Just in case. Mother Nature isn't the only one that doesn't like surprises.

3) D-I-Y

• Try first to locate freezer storage place within acceptable distance of your camp.

• If no freezer can be located, find a source of dry ice within range.

• Use bags of regular ice in a cooler to keep meat fresh and cool, but DO NOT let ice melt on meat.

Note: If you're near water, double-wrap the hide in securely sealed plastic bags and sink them to an appropriate depth in the water. Be careful there is no scent that could attract snapping turtles.

• Salt the hide when no cooling is available. When hide is dry, roll it and keep it cool (in shade, wrapped in an old sleeping bag, for instance). Wrap in a bag and put in cooler for transportation home.

Time to Get to Work...

After the bear is skinned, remove all excess meat, fat and other non-skin tissue from the hide. Then lay the hide flat on a tarp (to keep the hide cleaner) with fleshed side up. Be sure the hide has no wrinkles hiding unwanted materials. Then review your fleshing job to be sure you removed every bit of meat, fat and other unwanted tissue.

Now begin to prepare the hide for the trip home. Freeze the hide or salt it, but never both! A salted hide, rolled up and placed in a freezer, will not freeze. The salt prevents freezing; it dries the hide but holds heat. You can, however, use both processes with great results.

Salt the hide. Some people use canning salt; some say any fine or medium salt is fine. (Be sure to bring enough with you.) Rub salt into the hide, covering every bit of hide. Leave the hide on the tarp. The salt will soon become moist. At this point, remove the damp salt and re-salt the hide. Continue this remove/add process until the salt remains dry. Then roll up the hide, flesh side in, and place it in a bag.

I don't use plastic bags because I don't want to take a chance. I want the bag to permit airflow. Feed mill bags, the kind used to hold shelled corn and other grains, work very well. Any strong, breathable-fabric bag will work well.

Meat storage when no freezer is available

Bring a couple of large coolers (the largest storage capacity) and enough plastic to line them. The plastic keeps the cooler interior cleaner, of course. Bring regular ice or dry ice with you and keep it in good condition in the closed coolers in the coolest area you can find. (Anchoring in a nearby creek or lake, as deeply as possible without water leaking in?) If ice/dry ice is readily available in a nearby town, get it when you need it to minimize melting/vaporizing.

If you use regular ice, leave it in the bag to prevent melting ice from directly contacting meat or hide. Change ice often. Locate the nearest-to-camp gas stations or liquor stores (force yourself!) so you know where to get regular ice while you're in camp. On your drive home, you should see plenty of gas stations with ice. Do NOT let melted ice water touch meat because water contact will begin meat degradation.

Bone all meat. It will cool faster deboned and obviously takes less space in the coolers. If you want to bag the meat, leave the bags open overnight so the meat can cool better, then close the cooler lids and cover them with an old sleeping bag (which you will have placed on your planning list and then brought with you) in the shade or put in cool lake or river water.

On remote DIY hunts, there may be no freezer to use and no ice available. Salt the hide, let meat cool several hours and put it in the high quality coolers you will have brought, along with a few bags of ice you bought on the way. Leave for home as soon as you can and hope for the best until you can get more bagged ice.

"In a Perfect World" Freezing Hide and Meat

This will include a two-wheel utility trailer, a small chest freezer and a generator. A trailer large enough to hold all your gear is ideal. This keeps everything scent free and easily accessible while hunting. The bed of a pickup truck can work well, too, if there is enough space.

The freezer rests in the nose of the trailer. A small hole in the nose of the trailer allows easy extension cord hookup between freezer and generator or camp electrical source. This allows instant skinning and processing of meat and hide when that pleasant situation arises. This allows you to cut the meat the way you want. One other great factor -- I have never encountered an outfitter who does not like having a hunter take care of his own bear.

Hide

Line the freezer with a plastic drop cloth and place the hide in it, flesh side up, and leave for 12 hours. By keeping the hide open for the day or overnight, the hide cools adequately. DO NOT roll up the hide and place it in the freezer; the center of the hide will not freeze, giving bacteria and retained heat a chance to ruin the hide.

After those 12 hours, roll the stiff hide into a breathable bag, such as a feedbag or any strong woven bag, and place it in the freezer.

This attention to detail is important. If hide or meat is ruined, you have nothing but mixed memories. Never leave anything to chance. The extra time spent handling meat and hide properly will make good meals and a taxidermy mount or rug that will bring a lifetime of the right kind of memories.

Meat

Quarter and bone out the meat. Place it in the freezer on a tarp and let it cool a few hours before placing it in breathable bags. If you take your bear any day before the last day, cut up the bear and put it in vacuum-sealed bags with the amount of meat for one meal in each bag. Place the meat in the freezer and be darned sure the freezer is plugged in and working. You now have your own version of meals on wheels.

In early September 2013, I shot the biggest bear of my life, right in my home state of Wisconsin. The bear weighed more than 500 pounds. We needed to take care of it immediately because of the heat. We registered the bear (required in Wisconsin) and bought a boatload of ice, then filled the bear's chest cavity with bags of ice and piled several bags around its head. Those areas are where hair slippage usually starts. Then we headed home, at the speed limit.

Total time from shooting the bear to loading it into the cooler at home was around two hours. Did we need to be so cautious? Maybe, maybe not, but bet your life I always side with caution. It was a struggle to move the bear into the walk-in cooler, but we got it done as quickly as possible. We took photos then began taking care of hide and meat.

Tracking and properly processing your bear is as much a part of the hunt as shooting the bear. Be well prepared and you will preserve great memories and insure delicious meals.

Everyone always seems to have the hunting part under control, but many fail terribly on the post-hunt items. Be sure to plan everything from leaving home to returning home. You owe it to the bear, to yourself and to sport hunting.

A taxidermist advises...

Basics
Once the bear is down, skin it, flesh the skin, then salt down the entire hide with any kind of medium to fine salt.
- Let the salted hide lie on a clean spot on the ground or grass for a day, then hang it up the next day to drip out and drain. It won't hurt for moisture to pool on the hide after being salted, because you will hang it up to drain soon. Laying it out just insures some of the salt doesn't run off before taking effect.
- If freezer facilities are available, double-wrap the skin in two plastic bags with knots tied to seal them (for a salted hide that has had time to drain out), and place the package in a freezer until it can be taken to your taxidermist.
- If no freezer is present, skin the bear and flesh it, then salt down the entire hide with any kind of medium to fine salt. Then bag and wrap it.

Skinning a bear for rug or life-size mount:
1) Incisions
- Make an incision about four inches back from tip end of chin, underneath the chin and cut all the way to about three inches in front of the anus.
- Cut from paw to paw on front legs and paw to paw on back legs, starting from the footpad until you reach the center incision. On male bears, on the center incision, when reaching the scrotum cut down either side, leaving the scrotum intact.
- Leave ankles and wrists and paws on, so whoever skins out the feet

will have something to hold onto while cutting and pulling out wrist, ankle and toe bones. The skinning incision can be made at the bottom of the pad where it meets the hair, so you're not cutting through the pad.

If you don't have experience, skin down to toes as best you can and salt heavily.

2) Skinning
Option 1
• Upon reaching the feet, cut rear and front feet off underneath the skin at ankles and wrist joints, leaving them in paws and paws attached to the leg skin.

• Free hide from body.

• After bear is skinned, as part of fleshing make incision on underside of tail and remove the tailbone, from tip of tail to point where bone meets body.

• Once all legs are free, carefully remove the skin from the head. Take particular care around the eyes, nose, lips and ears.

• Flesh the hide of the head/face, including turning inside out the skin around the eyes and on the nose, lips and ears.

Skinning is now complete.

Option 2
• On a life-size mount, cut up the back, from behind the ears down to a few inches in front of the tail, then skin away from the body, until down to the legs. Make the leg incision only from elbows/knees down to the pads.

• Once you have skinned down to legs and have reached the leg incision, remove legs from ankle or wrist joint as in Option 1.

• After bear is skinned, as part of fleshing make incision on underside of tail and remove the tailbone, from tip of tail to point where bone meets body.

Skinning is now complete.

This method is good because it permits options on the posing of the full body mount.

Cutting the hide for shoulder mount or half-body mount:
• Shoulder mount -- cut a ring around the bear at least 10 inches behind the shoulder.

• Half-body mount -- cut a ring around the bear halfway between the animal's butt end and the middle of the body.

2) Follow-up
• If you salt the hide, it is best to remove all toe bones from feet. This is a job best left to experienced skinners and fleshers.

• Flesh the hide of the head/face, including turning inside out the skin around the eyes and on the nose, lips and ears.

• Flesh the remainder of the hide – neck, body, legs.

• Coat the entire exposed flesh part of the hide in salt, lay the entire hide flat, flesh side up, for a day, then hang it and allow it to drain a day or so before bagging up.

• *Work begins quickly after the kill.*

• *Every bit of fat and tissue comes off the hide during fleshing. Draping it over a big log helps focus efforts on a narrow area and keeps the remainder of the hide out of the way.*

• *Lay out the hide on a big tarp and salt, salt, salt every square inch of it.*

• *After the hide lays flat a day or so to let salt draw out liquids, hang it up and let it drip dry a day. Check the hide and salt again anywhere salting is needed.*

• *Stripping the feet is not an easy job. It's best left to an expert, unless you want to tackle it yourself. If you leave the job to the taxidermist, rub salt into all parts of the ankles/wrists. If you do the job yourself, cut carefully. The black objects on the skinned-out feet are foot pads.*

Remember these...

- There are the two ways to skin a bear for a life mount, as noted above.
- You have two ways to take care of the hide – freezing or salting. A frozen bear will last in a cooler several days <u>if completely frozen and rolled in a ball</u>.

Tip: The Butts prefer a drop-point knife for skinning. They use a Victorinox paring knife fleshing face and feet, and a big, fat, curved blade for fleshing the body.

Source: Chris & Foster Butt, Wildlife Taxidermy, Madison, TN

Care of Meat & Hide

CHAPTER 10 - *Memoir*
INTRODUCTION TO BEAR HUNTING WITH DOGS

I had always been negative about hunting bears with dogs, just did not like the whole picture. One fall, in fact the first year the lottery system began in Wisconsin, I drew a tag. Hound hunters went first that year; stand sitters waited until the second week. A friend near Superior, Wisconsin, was baiting a stand for me. I was excited to get north to hunt.

About a month prior to the bear hunt, an Ontario outfitter friend called. He had a cancellation on a moose hunt. With the short notice, he offered the hunt for only the price of the tag. Problem here: the week of my bear hunt was the same week as the moose hunt. I said I would get back to him.

While calling on a customer in Spooner, Wisconsin, I mentioned my dilemma and my less-than-enthusiastic outlook on hunting bears with dogs. My customer said he might have a solution regarding the dog issue.

He placed a phone call and within ten minutes a friend of his named Mike Stoner came to the shop. Mike talked to me about going with him and his group to hunt with dogs for bear. He also explained that if at anytime I thought what they did was not ethical, I could simply leave. I agreed. Also involved on that first dog hunt was Mike's good friend Dale Stafford, another dog man who had been hunting bear and bobcats with Mike for years.

That sounded interesting, so I took him up on his offer. The moose hunt would have to wait.

My feelings about dogs did not change much as we entered the first morning of the hunt. The three am start was a little harsh, but I was there to join in on my first dog hunt for bear. Mike went in one direction, Dale in the other, checking baits. They use the same baits bait watchers use, placing them close to logging roads or two-tracks and checking them pre-dawn instead of morning or mid-day.

If a bait was hit, they analyzed it to determine the size of the bear. Some hound hunters use sand around the bait to get a bear track image they can evaluate, others use frying grease. Grease seems to be a 4-to-1 favorite, probably because it has a bear-attracting aroma and can double as a bait. After the baits were checked, they met and decided which bear to hunt.

I was on deck as the second shooter. Another hunter, a young guy, was up first. As we drove to the bait we planned to hunt, the fellow who was to go on the first chase got ready. Mike and Dale each grabbed a dog and walked them to the bait. Soon their barks rang out as they started to trail the scent of a bear. After a short wait, Mike shouted "jumped". Three more dogs were let go and the chase was on. In less than five minutes I heard someone shout "treed". We walked in maybe 200 yards along an oak ridge, and there was the bear, about 25 feet up a big oak tree. The dogs were put on leashes and the young man put into position to shoot. A single shot brought the big bear out of the tree and a happy young bear hunter claimed his trophy.

Photos: Bill Wiesner

• *The three am start was a little harsh, but I was there to join in on my first dog hunt for bear.*

• *We walked in on an oak ridge, and there was the bear, about 25 feet up a big oak tree.*

That was too easy. I was still on the fence about this dog hunting when Dale told me the next chase was mine. They decided to go to a bait where they had seen a good-sized track. Once there, the dogs were turned loose again. (My wife Sandy and two sons Brad and Bryan were along to witness dad's first hound hunt.)

Soon, once again, the song of hounds barking said "jumped". Dale, Mike and my two sons monitored the dogs' movement on tracking systems, and soon grabbed their gear. All four of them headed into the woods.

Dale had given me a hand-held radio and said "Turn it to channel seven and be ready."

The dogs soon were out of hearing distance. Sandy and I sat in my truck, munched doughnuts and drank coffee. I guess this wasn't so bad; maybe I could get to like hunting bears with dogs. However, that routine didn't last.

A voice came over the radio. "Hey, Dad, you got a copy? The bear is treed. Come on in. Just follow the ridge to the first swamp, cross the river and go straight north to the second swamp. You will go over two oak ridges go over two oak ridges on your way. Stop then and listen for the dogs."

Following the ridge was no problem. The river, however, had ten feet of soupy, black swamp muck on each side before the high banks. I waded through the muck, crossed the river and battled the muck on the other side. Great fun! Of course, Sandy was filming all this for later family enjoyment.

Just as I sat on a stump to catch my breath, Bryan's voice came over the radio. "You going to get here before the season closes?" Ya ya ya!

I got back underway and could hear the faint sound of dogs howling. Their voices rang louder as I moved from second ridge to second swamp. Finally…gasp, wheeze…I caught sight of my crew standing around a large hemlock tree looking up, and I could see a black image about 25 feet up the tree. After catching my breath, I double-lunged the bear, with my arrow disappearing through the bear and flying unseen into the swamp. My first hound hunt was complete, or so I thought.

It took all of us the better part of five hours to get that bear out of the woods.

The bear weighed about 275 pounds and seemed to weigh over 500 pounds before we reached the road. It was carried on a large pole with its legs tied to the pole. Sometimes a bear sways side to side when carried this way and tends to assume command, rocking the bearers back and forth. This one didn't, fortunately, but many times the bearers had to set it down, then physically lift it over brush and downed trees.

Dogs were walked out on leads. Whoever wasn't carrying the bear had to hold onto dogs.

Photo: Bill Wiesner

- *We – I say 'we' because this was a hunt with hounds and hound men, which means they were in charge and it was a cooperative effort – took this bear on a hunt near Spooner, Wisconsin. I hunted with Mike Stoner, Dale Stafford and Dale Stafford Jr. This was my first hunt with hounds. It was an eye-opening experience.*

We took the clearest route even if we had to go out of our way to walk (or stagger) around downed trees, potholes and thick brush. The terrain was hilly with several swamp bottoms that really worked us. We switched off bearers regularly, so all could get a breather once in a while. We handed it over potholes. We stopped often so everyone could take five.

At the river, we slid that big carcass as best we could through the swamp muck, then floated it on open water to the other side and slid it through that muck.

The bear had to be cleaned up before we could begin butchering it, and we all needed a shower. We were tired, muddy and sweaty. The bear was just muddy.

At six feet and more than 300 pounds, there's a good chance I was more exhausted than anyone.

My attitude on hound hunting was adjusted, and it didn't even include mountains!

CHAPTER 10 - How-To
BEAR ON THE TABLE

Many people consider bear meat undesirable for consumption. Wrong, wrong, wrong. But, as with all wild game, it does depend upon how well you handle the carcass in the field and in butchering, processing, freezing, thawing and cooking.

I also render bear fat for making piecrusts and for waterproofing my leather boots.

WRAPPING & FREEZING
Wrapping
1) Make each package good for one meal only. Put a piece of waxed paper between individual cuts of meat. They will thaw better later and not freeze together. Packages with more than one meal of meat lead to lowered quality due to thawing and then refreezing the unused portion.

2) Best wrapping, requiring only one layer of wrapping material, is done by the automatic vacuum wrap machines which suck oxygen from the package, then heat seal the package air tight.

If you use plastic bags and wrapping paper, wrap the plastic bag around a soda straw, suck the air from the package, twist the bag just below the lower end of the straw and seal the bag with a wire twist. Then wrap the plastic

Photo: Glenn Helgeland

• *Vacuum-sealing removes air from the package, enabling the meat to remain high quality longer. Only one package layer is needed, as opposed to the double-wrapping of packages wrapped by hand.*

bag in heavy freezer paper, shiny side in, and seal with masking tape.

Any good sealed wrap will prevent moisture loss for normal storage time. "Freezer burn" is excessive moisture loss, drying and hardening of meat. Meat with freezer burn turns white on the surface.

Freezing

Flash freezing is best, by far, because the ice crystals which form in the moisture in the meat remain small. When meat freezes slowly, the ice crystals are large. Larger crystals cause the cells to break down, increasing water loss and creating a mushier piece of meat when it is thawed for cooklng.

Flash freezing needs an internal freezer temperature of minus-10 degrees Fahrenheit. Frozen meat stores best at 0 degrees F.

Meat flash freezes best when it is thoroughly chilled first. Use your refrigerator or a cold garage to do this part, then freeze it.

When you place meat in the freezer for flash freezing, place the packages close to the freezer walls, where temperatures are coolest, and keep the packages from touching each other. This gives best air circulation and thus best freezing. After the packages are frozen they can be repositioned for best storage.

How long can meat be kept frozen without losing quality? General rule of thumb with most venison is six to eight months, with sausages having a slightly shorter time and large roasts and steaks slightly longer.

Since bear meat can be greasier than venison, and thus likely to become rancid sooner, as with sausage, it's probably best to stick with a short storage time with bear meat.

Rules & Tips

1) Any recipe you like for beef or venison also will work well with bear meat.

2) As with venison, it's important to bone out all meat for packaging, and trim all fat from bear meat before cooking, plus as much connective tissue and muscle sheathing as possible. Bear meat can be greasy, making fat trimming especially important, because it can turn rancid quickly if not trimmed properly and stored properly. The other two items can add a strong or 'gamey' flavor and resist all chewing efforts.

3) Cook bear meat until well done, being sure to get internal temperature to 170 degrees F. Bears can have and transmit trichinosis. Temps of 170 degrees F or higher kills all trichina parasites that may be in the meat, but try to stay under 200 degrees F so the meat doesn't get dry and crispy. Trichinosis affects the joints and is painful.

4) Best bear meat comes from hams and loins. Meat from front legs, neck and shoulders usually is ground for hamburger or cubed for stews and stir-fry.

5) A sharp knife is invaluable any time you're butchering meat, but especially so when working with small, sometimes hard-to-handle, sometimes tough pieces of meat. Have a hard steel handy and use it often to keep your knife blade sharp. A sharp blade cuts with little or no pressure; a dull blade must be pushed and thus is more likely to slip and cut you.

6) When covering food with aluminum foil for cooking, cover or wrap with dull side of foil out. This shortens cooking time because the dull foil

• Butchering a bear is a lighter, faster job when the entire gang pitches in, and the meat will be ready for cooling sooner.

Photos: Glenn Helgeland

• Good steel, used frequently, keeps a knife blade sharp...and safe... because it cuts easily. A dull blade must be pushed and can slip.

side absorbs heat. (Shiny side reflects heat.)

7) Bone out as much meat as you can. Meat cooks slower close to bone, producing uneven doneness levels throughout the entire piece. Boneless meat cooks more evenly.

8) Never add salt until after cooking to avoid dehydration of the meat. Season meat as little as possible for best taste.

9) Do not soak wild game meat in baking soda or salt water. Doing so dries the meat, making it a good shoe leather candidate.

10) Fast heat searing helps meat hold moisture.

TWO METHODS OF MEAT COOKING

Dry heat: Roasting, broiling, pan broiling, frying. Use roasting for round, loin and shoulder, broiling or frying for more tender steaks and chops.

Moist heat: Braising, stewing, pressure-cooking, crockpot. Use moist heat for shoulder, neck, brisket, rump, round, shank and flank.

Dry heat methods are preferred for cooking the kinds and cuts of meat that are naturally tender. Moist heat is preferred for the less tender meats, as it helps to soften the connective tissue.

Cooking Tip: When substituting dry herbs for fresh herbs in a recipe, use half the amount recommended. Dry herbs are more concentrated. Conversely, when substituting fresh herbs for dry herbs, double the amount called for. Most recipes in any cookbook are written for dry herbs.

BLACK BEAR MEAT Nutritional Value
Nutritional value per 100 grams (3.5 oz.)

Energy   649 kj (155 calories)
  Carbohydrates   0.00 g
  Fat   8.30 g
  Protein   20.10 g

• Percentages are roughly approximated using U.S. recommendations for adults.
• Source: USDA Nutrient Data

Vitamins

Vitamin A equiv.	10%	78 mg	
Thiamine (B1)	14%	0.160 mg	
Riboflavin (B2)	57%	0.680 mg	
Niacin (B3)	21%	3.20 mg	

Trace Minerals

Iron	55%	7.20 mg
Phosphorus	23%	162 mg

Water   72.20 g

Units
- ug = micrograms
- mg = milligrams
- IU = International Units

TABLE OF MEASUREMENTS

C	=	**Cup**
Tbl	=	**Tablespoon**
Tsp	=	**Teaspoon**
Lb	=	**Pound**
Oz	=	**Ounce**

MARINADES & MARINATING

Some of you may find bear meat to have a slightly strong taste; others will not. If there is a stronger taste than you prefer, marinating the meat will add a flavor you like. There are several options.

• Any acid-based liquid will make a good marinade, such as the juice from several citrus fruits, tomato or pineapple juice, milk or wine.

Photos: Glenn Helgeland

• Any acid-based liquid will work, such as a weak vinegar-water solution (1 cup vinegar to 1 gallon water) and milk, plus citric juices (orange, lemon, lime, grapefruit, clementines, tangerines), tomato juice, Italian salad dressing. Tomato juice will neutralize strong odors. The naturally high acidic content of tomato juice also helps tenderize meat.

Many berries, except blueberries, contain naturally-occurring citric acid. Berries with higher amounts of citric acid include strawberries, raspberries, cranberries, red and black currants, and gooseberries.

Pineapple contains citric acid. Stone fruits, such as cherries, peaches and apricots, also contain citric acid.

• After it is marinated, cook bear meat as you would beef. As with most cooking, a bit of experimentation may be necessary to find the preparation methods, marinades and recipes you prefer.

• Be sure not to overcook the meat. Bear meat and pork are the only meats that must be cooked to an internal temperature of 170 degrees F., which makes them well done (not the same as overcooked) to eliminate the possibility of trichinosis.

Wine Is Fine

Wine works well in many wild game recipes (and in many wild game cooks). Wine can be a meat tenderizer in a meat marinade, or it can be a seasoning. Wine is as easy to use as salt and pepper, and it brings food flavors together in interesting ways. The alcohol evaporates as the wine cooks, leaving only the fine flavor. So it can be used in any family recipe.

To use wine in recipes that don't call for it, just substitute it for part of the other liquids called for.

Use a good table wine in your cooking instead of a cooking wine. You will like the results better. Red meats can be cooked with red wines; they generally have richer or more robust flavors.

Marinating Notes:

1) If a marinade is used on meat and drained off, then reused to baste the meat during cooking, the marinade must be heated to the boiling point for 1-2 minutes before it is reused. Bacteria from the meat could be in the marinade and make it unsafe if it isn't reheated.

2) No matter which marinade you use, cover the meat and refrigerate it for the entire marinating process.

3) Foods can be marinated up to 48 hours, but 24 hours usually is long enough for the marinade to penetrate the meat, thus adding flavor. Marinate meat at least 4 hours; 8 hours is better. When using commercial marinades, follow instructions on the package.

4) Do not cut chops or steaks until ready to marinate or cook. Any cut creates water loss from the meat; thus, the earlier the cuts, the more the meat will have dried before you're ready to work with it.

MARINADE FOR POT ROAST

- ½ C. olive oil
- 2 C. beef broth
- 1 med. onion, sliced
- venison roast
- ¼ C. vinegar
- 2 C. wine
- 2 cloves garlic, minced
- few sprigs fresh parsley
- 1 tsp. celery seed
- 2 carrots, chopped
- 8 peppercorns
- 2 stalks celery, chopped with leaves

Mix above ingredients; pour over roast in large non-metal bowl or zip-lock bag (nice to use because you can stir and mix without getting your hands dirty). Marinate for 4-24 hours in the refrigerator. Remove meat and vegetables from marinade and discard marinade. Roll meat in flour seasoned with pepper. Brown meat on all sides in hot vegetable oil. Place roast and vegetables in roasting pan, cover and roast at 425° 10-12 minutes per pound.

Note: Marinade can also be used for chops and other cuts of meat.

RED WINE MARINADE

Mix 1 cup dry red wine, 2 cloves garlic, 2 tbsp. white vinegar, 1 cup cooking oil and 1 small onion (minced). Marinate a three-pound round steak overnight in a non-metal container, being sure the meat is covered, or turning it a couple of times. Grill the meat, brushing with marinade.

MEAT MARINADE
- ½ tsp. garlic powder per pound of meat
- Red wine

Rub garlic powder into meat. Place meat in a container and cover meat with red wine. If desired (with tough meat), use meat tenderizer as directed in the marinade. Cover and refrigerate for eight or more hours, or overnight.

When grilling the meat after marinating, use the marinade liquid to baste the meat. You can also use this marinade when roasting meat in a Dutch oven. It does wonders to and for meat.

* * * * * * * * * *

RECIPES...RECIPES...RECIPES

BEAR CHIPS JERKY
The best bear jerky comes from a roast. Thaw the roast to about 75% completion; it cuts well at this slightly-frozen point. Slice the roast at least 1/8-inch thick, and ¼-inch wouldn't hurt. Place the sliced meat in a sealable plastic bag and cover it with seasoning of your choice. (We use Dale's brand, which can be found in most grocery stores in the Midwest or at www.dalesseasoning.com. It contains soy sauce, onion, garlic, sugar, MSG, ginger and paprika.)

Refrigerate for 12 hours, then wash off excess seasoning, pat meat dry with paper towels, then place it on dehydrator trays for 6-8 hours, checking every couple of hours for desired degree of doneness. When properly dried, remove jerky from dehydrator and cool in the refrigerator several hours. Then store it in a cool, airtight container, such as a former peanut butter jar with screw-on lid. Safest storage is in your refrigerator, especially for thicker meat slices, which may not have all moisture removed.

HASH BROWN STACKER BREAKFAST
- ½ pound bear Italian sausage
- Slice/chop/dice peppers, onions, mushrooms to taste
- Two serving size portions of hash browns

Cook vegetables and bear sausage. Place hash browns in frying pan or medium heat. As the hash browns are nearly fully cooked, place cooked vegetables and meat atop hash browns. Sprinkle on your favorite cheese; let it melt in. Place three eggs (over easy, fried, scrambled, however you prefer) atop everything when it is done. Serves 2.

- *We make this from bear hamburger with Italian seasoning added to taste. We usually make 10 pounds at a time and let the mixture sit overnight in the refrigerator. Then we package it into half-pound bags and freeze them*

GRILLED CHEESE/BEAR-BACON SANDWICH

Fry six pieces of bacon cut in half crosswise. This is enough for two sandwiches. Drain bacon on paper toweling while preparing remainder of sandwiches. Place sliced jalapeno-jack cheese and fried bacon strips between two slices of sourdough bread. Butter the outside of both bread slices, place in a greased pan on medium heat. Turn the sandwiches once to fry both sides evenly and melt the cheese.

• We have bear bacon made at our local meat market. If you cannot get a local meat market in your area to do this, you'll have to make your own bacon or substitute thick slices of regular pork bacon.

• The cheese can be found at www.renardscheese.com if you cannot find it locally.

CROCK POT DELIGHT

Before you leave for work in the morning, place a 2-4 pound frozen bear roast in a crockpot that has been sprayed with olive oil. Add a small amount of water. Mix two 10.5-ounce cans of cream of mushroom soup with one 10.5-ounce can of water, add one 10-ounce can of beef gravy. Stir mixture thoroughly, then pour over the roast. Place three thinly sliced apples atop the meat and soup mixture.

Set crockpot heat on medium and go to work. Your dinner will be ready when you get home. Check it immediately to avoid overcooking. Season to taste with seasoning salt and pepper when roast is served.

BEAR SWISS STEAK

Roll in flour 3 pounds of bear steak cut into 5-6 steaks. Pound both sides of floured steak with meat tenderizer hammer to help tenderize. Cover bottom of fry pan to ¼-inch depth with virgin olive oil. Set burner on high; as soon as olive oil begins to roll, drop in meat, turning once to brown both sides. Sprinkle one envelope of onion soup mix over meat as it browns. In a bowl, mix 1 10.5-ounce can of cream of mushroom soup with 1 10.5-ounce can of water. (Option: add two chopped tomatoes; tomatoes are acidic and will help tenderize meat.) Pour mixture over meat. Cover and bake at 350 degrees for 1½-2 hours. Serves 4-8.

BEAR STROGANOFF

Cube 1½ pounds of bear meat into 1-inch cubes. Roll cubed meat in flour and brown in one stick of melted butter in frying pan. Dissolve two beef bullion cubes in 1½ cups of hot water. Mix in 1 can cream of mushroom soup. Pour over meat. Add ½-1 cup chopped onions, and sliced, canned mushrooms to personal preference quantity (1-2 cups). Add 2–3 tbsp. of white wine. Simmer contents until meat is tender (1–2 hours), checking frequently after 1 hour. Add ½-¾ cup sour cream and heat 20 minutes more. Serve over rice, noodles or mashed potatoes. Serves 4.

BARBEQUE SAUCE

• 1 tbsp. butter or margarine
• 1 clove garlic, minced
• 1 tbsp. Worcestershire sauce
• 1 tbsp. prepared mustard

- 2 tbsp. chopped onion
- ½ C. catsup
- ½ C. chili sauce
- 2 tbsp. brown sugar
- 1 tsp. celery seed
- ¼ tsp. salt
- dash hot pepper sauce
- 1 tbsp. lemon juice

In saucepan, melt butter or margarine, add garlic and onion and cook 1-2 minutes. Add remaining ingredients and bring to a boil. Yields 2 cups.

SIX-IN-ONE
- 1 to 1-1/2 pounds ground meat
- 1 to 1-1/2 C. uncooked minute rice
- 3 carrots, diced
- 3 stalks celery, diced
- 1 small onion, diced
- 2-3 C. stewed tomatoes

Brown ground meat and place in bottom of 4-quart casserole. Add succeeding layers of uncooked rice, carrots, celery, onion and top with stewed tomatoes. Add 1 cup water. Cover and bake in a 300 degree F. oven for 3-4 hours, until rice and vegetables are tender. Serves 6.

- *This is visually appealing in a clear glass casserole. The layered ingredients are distinct and colorful.*

YOGURT MEAT KABOBS
Add 1 tsp. salt, a pinch of pepper and ½ tsp. ginger to 2 cups yogurt. Cube 1-1/2 pounds steak. Marinate in seasoning mixture for 1 hour. Thread meat onto skewers, alternating with cherry tomatoes, mushroom caps, small onions and red/green/yellow/pepper chunks. Sprinkle with ginger. Broil until desired doneness is obtained, basting occasionally with melted butter or margarine. Serves 4-6.

CANNED RAW MEAT
Pack raw meat pieces (1 to 1-1/2 inch cubes) into jars. Fill to 1 inch from the top. Add 1 tsp. salt per quart and a little pepper. You won't need to add any liquid because it will make its own when cooked. Screw on lids and process in pressure cooker – pints 1-1/4 hours and quarts 1-1/2 hours – at 10 pounds of pressure.

BEAR PAW LANDING BEAR ROAST
Pieces may be tied together with string to give a rolled roast effect. Marinate for about 12 hours in a solution of 1 cup vinegar to 1 gallon water. Rinse thoroughly in cool water before roasting. Place roast in roasting pan. Add a dash of garlic powder. Cover and roast at 350 degrees until well done. Salt and pepper to individual preferences when served. Variation: Add water to the roasting pan with a packaged beef-mushroom mix or onion soup mix, which makes its own tasty gravy.

BEAR LOIN
Marinate a 4-1/2 lb. slice of bear loin in your favorite marinade 24 hours, then rinse and dry well. Rub a mashed clove of garlic on a heated platter. Make a paste of 3 tbsp. butter or margarine, 3 tbsp. finely minced chives, 1 generous tbsp. French mustard, 1-1/2 tbsp. tomato paste, and a dash of Worcestershire sauce. Cover the platter with this paste and add a thick late

of sliced onions covered with butter or margarine. Season with ½ tsp. salt, pepper and a little paprika. Keep the platter hot.

Sear bear loin well on both sides under a high oven broiler flame or over a grill.

Reduce the flame and broil meat as desired to 170 degrees, basting frequently with melted butter or margarine. Dust the loin with salt and pepper and serve on the platter topped with mushroom caps sautéed in brown butter or margarine and a sprinkle of chopped parsley.

Howard Thelemann

BIG GAME ROAST
- 2 lb. roast (bear, or any venison)
- 1 (10-1/2 oz.) can consommé
- ½ C. white or red wine, preferably red wine

Place roast in Dutch oven and add consommé and wine. Roast slowly in a 250-degree oven 3-4 hours until roast is tender. Serves 6.

MEATLOAF
- 2 lbs. ground bear or other venison
- 2 lbs. bulk pork sausage
- 2 medium onions, chopped fine
- 1-1/2 C. cracker crumbs
- 1 C. evaporated milk
- 3 eggs, slightly beaten
- 2 C. barbeque sauce
- 1 tsp. salt
- ½ tsp. fresh ground pepper

Place wild game meat, sausage, onion and cracker crumbs in large bowl. Mix well. Add milk, eggs, 1 cup barbeque sauce, salt and pepper. Blend well. Chill 15 minutes. Shape into 2 loaves; place in large greased baking pans. Bake in preheated 350-degree oven for 30 minutes. Spoon remaining barbeque sauce over loaves and bake 45 minutes more. Serves 8-10.

MARINATED ROUND STEAK
Marinate meat (1 to 1-1/2 pounds) in mixture of 4 tbsp. soy sauce, 2 tbsp. cooking oil, 2 tbsp. Worcestershire sauce, juice of ½ lemon, 4 tbsp. wine vinegar and 1 crushed garlic clove. Marinate overnight, turning once or twice, in refrigerator. Cook slowly in electric skillet at 275 degrees with ¼-pound bacon or use ¼-cup bacon fat, turning once and cooking until done, about 45 minutes. If animal is young there is no need to marinate. Serves 4-6.

LEFTOVER ROAST BBQ
Chop 1 medium onion. Saute` in 3 tbsp. butter or margarine. Add 1-1/2 pounds meat and ½ cup prepared chili sauce. Simmer 15 minutes and serve.

BEER BEAR STEW 1
3 lbs. bear roast
1 bottle Mesquite Marinade
  with Lime Juice
1 (10 oz.) pkg. frozen peas
2 tsp. garlic powder
- 2 lbs. potatoes, diced
- 2 C. sliced carrots
- 2 C. diced celery
- 2 onions, cut into wedges
- 1 (12 oz.) can of beer

with parsley
- 1 (1 oz.) pkg. brown gravy mix
- 2 tbsp. parsley, finely chopped
- 2 tsp. seasoned salt
- 1 tsp. seasoned pepper

Place venison, onion, celery, carrots, mesquite marinade, beer, seasoned salt, garlic and seasoned pepper in 3-quart crockpot. Set on low and cook at least 8 hours and up to 36 hours until meat is tender. Add additional water or beer if needed. The last 2 hours of cooking time, raise cooking temperature to medium or high, add gravy mix, potatoes, peas and parsley. Serves 8.

- *Beer tenderizes the meat. All alcohol is evaporated in the cooking process. If you don't have a crockpot, use a Dutch oven and cook on top of stove, or use a pressure cooker. Substitute your favorite or seasonal vegetables as you wish.*

BEER BEAR STEW 2
- 1-1/2 lbs. bear roast, cut into 1/2-inch pieces
- 1-1/2 C. water
- 4 (4.5 oz.) packets instant beef flavor broth mix
- 1 tbsp. brown sugar, packed
- 1 bay leaf
- ½ C. cauliflower pieces
- 2 tbsp. vegetable oil
- ¾ C. beer
- 1 tbsp. onion, diced
- ¼ tsp. ground thyme
- 1 (16 oz.) can sliced carrots
- ½ C. frozen peas
- ¼ C. all-purpose flour
- ¾ C. water

Cut meat into ½-inch pieces. Brown meat in oil over medium-high heat in Dutch oven. Add water, beer, broth, onion, brown sugar, thyme and bay leaf. Reduce heat; cover. Simmer until meat is tender, approximately 1-1/2 hours, stirring occasionally. Add carrots, cauliflower and peas. Cook 15 minutes. Remove bay leaf and discard. Add flour mixed with ¾ cup water. Cook 10 minutes or until thickened. Serves 6-8.

GLENN HELGELAND: EDITOR / PUBLISHER

Target Communications Outdoor Books has now published 17 titles in its "On Target" series, with subjects on archery, bowhunting, deer hunting, muzzleloader shooting, wild game cooking and, now, black bear hunting.

Glenn Helgeland, editor and publisher of this book, has been a magazine and book editor and publisher since 1968. He was editor/associate publisher of *ARCHERY WORLD* (now *BOWHUNTING WORLD*) consumer magazine from 1970 to 1980.. He won awards from the National Archery Association for service to archery and from the National Shooting Sports Foundation for a series of articles titled "The Hunter's Story".

He was the founding editor and associate publisher of *ARCHERY RETAILER* (now *ARCHERY BUSINESS*) trade magazine.

Before becoming involved in archery/bowhunting writing and publishing, Helgeland was associate editor of *NATIONAL WILDLIFE* magazine.

He has been, at various times, bowhunting columnist for *FINS & FEATHERS, AMERICAN HUNTER, NORTH AMERICAN HUNTER* and *BOWHUNTING WORLD* magazines, and a marketing and sales promotion columnist for *ARCHERY BUSINESS*.

Helgeland co-authored with John Williams, men's 1972 Olympic archery gold medalist, the book "Archery For Beginners". He also edited the 2nd edition of the Pope and Young Club's Big Game Records Book.

His previous company (Target Communications Corporation, founded in 1980) owned and produced deer and turkey hunting expositions in Wisconsin, Michigan, Ohio, Illinois and Tennessee from 1985 through 2011. He sold the expos to Bonnier Corp. in 2011. Bonnier publishes Field & Stream and Outdoor Life magazines.

He is a member of the Professional Outdoor Communicators Association (POMA).

Glenn also is a long-time bear hunter, doing his own scouting and baiting, and hunting with outfitters. He has hunted black bear in Wisconsin, Minnesota, Idaho, Ontario, Manitoba, Alberta and Saskatchewan. The ten bears he has tagged were taken with bow and arrow. One qualified for the Pope & Young Club record book. He has taken black, cinnamon and tri-color color phases of black bear; his goal is to take all color phases.

Photo: Glenn Helgeland

• **Glenn Helgeland with a northern Alberta bear that twice checked out his treestand to make sure he stayed in it, ran a smaller bear off the bait pile and checked out the outfitter's baiting trail before getting in the way of an arrow.**

The "On Target" Series of Outdoor Books
from Target Communications

UNDERSTANDING WINNING ARCHERY, Hall of Fame Commemorative Edition, by Al Henderson, coach of the 1976 U.S. Olympic Archery Team. Mental control means better shooting results, easier archery gear set-up and tuning, more-productive practices, and winning archer – target, field and hunting.

122 pages. ISBN: 0-913305-20-0. $12.95

TAKING TROPHY WHITETAILS, by Bob Fratzke with Glenn Helgeland. In-depth, detailed information on year-round scouting, and its huge payoff, scrape hunting, rut hunting,, late-season hunting, camo, use of scents, mock scrapes and licking branches.

140 pages. ISBN: 0-913305-02-2. $10.95

TO HECK WITH GRAVY wild game cookbook, by Glenn & Judy Helgeland. Great meals from quick, easy recipes; don't be tied to the kitchen. Includes 209 recipes – roasts, steaks, marinades, soups/stews, ground meat, fish, birds. Plus field dressing, meat handling/processing tips, spice charts, low sodium diet tips.

120 pages. ISBN: 0-913305-05-7. $12.95

TASTY JERKY RECIPES, by Glenn & Judy Helgeland. Spicy, mild, sweet and no-sodium recipes for three meat cut thicknesses and tendernesses; gives three different tastes for each recipe.

$2.00 plus stamped, self-addressed #10 return envelope.

TUNING YOUR COMPOUND BOW (4th Edition), by Larry Wise. If you shoot a compound bow, this book belongs in your tackle box! Round wheel, single cam and super cam set-up and tuning chapters, making/serving/repairing strings and cables, pre-use bow preparation, draw stroke, power stroke, shooting from the valley, fine tuning, test shooting, tuning fast-flight cable systems, building and tuning aluminum and carbon arrows. Includes a chapter on asymmetrical (hybrid) cams, an extensive chapter on 3D, tuning and shooting for bowhunting, and updated cam materials on all cam systems.

146 pages. ISBN: 0-913305-19-7. $13.95

TUNING & SILENCING YOUR BOWHUNTING SHOOTING SYSTEM (3rd Edition), by Larry Wise. Problem-solving info on fitting bow (compound, recurve, longbow) to your body style and shooting form; broadhead effects on arrow flight; noise reduction throughout entire system; aiming/shooting strategy; proper practice; plus much of the compound set-up and tuning info in Tuning Your Compound Bow.

170 pages. ISBN: 0-913305-16-2. $13.95

BECOME THE ARROW (The Art of Modern Barebow Shooting), by famed archery trick shot Byron Ferguson with Glenn Helgeland. Details the 'become the arrow' philosophy; explains how to visualize arrow flight path and sight picture; shooting form practice and mental exercises; tuning for barebow shooting, bowhunting details and more.

Book -- 112 pages. ISBN: 0-913305-09-X. $13.95
Video (VHS 45 minutes). UPC 8-29493-12467-9. $19.95

THE WILD PANTRY wild game cookbook, by Glenn & Judy Helgeland. 200-plus recipes (steaks, roasts, goulash, stews, Mexican, jerky, sausages (patties, links, summer, etc.); mostly venison, but upland birds, fish, waterfowl, too. You will enjoy the stories and anecdotes about wonderful (and some not-so-wonderful) wild game cooking experiences and meals.

156 pages. ISBN: 0913305-13-8. $12.95

CORE ARCHERY, by Larry Wise. Learn proper back tension and much more. This is a systematic set of shooting form steps built around the proper use of your skeleton. Throughout each form step, the governing theme is to maintain skeleton and minimize muscle effort for maximum efficiency. If you do this, your form will be energy efficient, fatigue resistant and highly repeatable.

128 pages. ISBN: 0-913305-18-9. $13.95

NEW! **THE BEAR HUNTING OBSESSION OF A DRIVEN MAN,** by Bill Wiesner Jr. and Glenn Helgeland. Ten hunting how-to chapters and 10 memoir chapters. How-to chapters include black bear natural history; distribution, population & record book entry totals (by state and province); hunting gear (rifle, slug gun, handgun, muzzleloader, bow, crossbow); camo, and other items; hunting from ground blinds; hunting styles (D-I-Y, guided, hounds, spot-and-stalk); scouting; baiting and scents; new twists (food plots, calling, decoying); the shot (before, during, after); care of hide for taxidermy; care of meat (processing, freezing, recipes).

172 pages. ISBN: 978-0-913305-11-9. $19.95

TO ORDER:
1) Go to your local sporting goods dealer or bookstore
2) Go to our website – www.targetcommbooks.com
3) Call 1-262-242-3530

Write, E-Mail or Call for a FREE Information Flyer and Order Form:
TARGET COMMUNICATIONS OUTDOOR BOOKS
10459 N. Wauwatosa Rd., Mequon, WI 53097
judy.helgeland@gmail.com / 262-242-3530